HARRIET TUBMAN

This republication of Sarah H. Bradford's memorable biography of Harriet Tubman is an exact, unaltered and unabridged, reprint of the expanded second edition of 1886. The first edition appeared in 1869. Both were privately printed by Mrs. Bradford for the purpose of raising funds to aid "the Moses of her people."

The famous portrait of Harriet Tubman on the cover appeared facing the title page of the first edition, *Scenes in the Life of Harriet Tubman.* It is reproduced from a copy in the Schomburg Collection of the New York Public Library with their kind permission.

HARRIET TUBMAN.

Harriet Tubman

THE MOSES OF HER PEOPLE

by Sarah Bradford

Introduction by Butler A. Jones

A Citadel Press Book
Published by Carol Publishing Group

BUTLER A. JONES is a graduate of Morehouse College, Atlanta, Ga., and received his Ph.D. in American Civilization at New York University. He was a consultant on the Carnegie-Myrdal Study of the Negro in the United States and has contributed to the scholarly journals, particularly in reference to the Negro in American civilization. He is presently Chairman of the Department of Sociology at Ohio Wesleyan University where he has been on the staff since 1952.

First Carol Publishing Group Edition 1991

A Citadel Press Book
Published by Carol Publishing Group

Editorial Offices   Sales & Distribution Offices
600 Madison Avenue   120 Enterprise Avenue
New York, NY 10022   Secaucus, NJ 07094

In Canada: Musson Book Company
A division of General Publishing Co. Limited
Don Mills, Ontario

Citadel Press is a registered trademark of
Carol Communications, Inc.

Manufactured in the United States of America
ISBN 0-8065-0415-3

15   14   13   12   11   10 9   8   7   6   5

Carol Publishing Group books are available at special discounts
for bulk purchases, for sales promotions, fund raising, or
educational purposes. Special editions can also be created to
specifications. For details contact: Special Sales Department,
Carol Publishing Group, 120 Enterprise Ave., Secaucus, NJ 07094

INTRODUCTION

Go down Moses! Way down in Egyptland!
Tell ol' Pharoah let my people go!

In such simple but dramatic language as this did the
slaves of the plantation South adapt the Jewish story as
told in Exodus to their own situation. For behind this
seemingly naive appeal for a Mosaic emissary to the slave
owners lay the slaves' firm belief that the slave masters'
refusal to heed the repeated urgings to "let my people
go" would eventually result in Divine deliverance. Had
it not been thus with the Children of Israel who, like the
slaves, had been put to labor in a foreign land? Could He
do less for these His children also? There were many who
in the years prior to 1860 undertook the Mosaic mission
and appealed to the plantation owners to abandon the
system of chattel slavery. There were those too who, tiring
of the apparent fruitlessness of these diplomatic missions,
took up the mantle of deliverer. Some of these were
notably unsuccessful (Nat Turner and John Brown, for
example) while others, relying upon more devious means,

were notably successful. Among these latter none was
more daring or individually successful than was Harriet
Tubman—the subject of this wholly sympathetic but revealing biography by Sarah Bradford.

This is an important book. Whatever its shortcomings as
an exercise in classical biography, the story told here is
an integral part of the events which a century ago led to
the great American excursion into fratricide. Those who
would dismiss the book on critical grounds should bear
in mind the fact that Harriet Tubman was not only an
illiterate, highly visible run-away slave but that she was
engaged in an illegal activity. Under the circumstances, it
should come as no surprise to discover that those who gave
her aid and comfort were not disposed to record that fact
in diary, memoir, or letter—traditional sources of biographi-
cal data. Such documentary evidence would have been fatal
to their defense if ever they were brought to trial for
aiding a fugitive slave to escape.

The book is not without documentation, however. In this
second edition Mrs. Bradford was prescient enough to in-
clude in text and appendix letters from, among others,
such noted anti-slavery leaders as Gerrit Smith and Thomas
Garret. These directly corroborate Harriet's version of
the exploits recorded here and lend support to the accu-
racy of her reports of other journeys into "Egypt-land."

While the subtitle of Mrs. Bradford's book (THE MO-
SES OF HER PEOPLE) is perhaps a more apt description
of Harriet's role in leading more than three hundred of her
kinsmen out of the land of bondage, in the male dominated
world of her contemporary admirers she was more com-
monly pictured as an American Joan of Arc. The similar-
ities between the two are interesting though perhaps not
especially revealing. Like Joan, Harriet was born among
the dispossessed, denied the rudiments of a formal edu-

cation, reared in a harsh social environment, early enveloped by a simple albeit compulsive religious faith, and was actively sought by the minions of the law because of the price on her head. Like Joan also she was harbored and supported by many persons willing to risk their all in furtherance of her cause. But unlike Joan whose name and deeds have since become a part of the formal learning experience of every Frenchman, neither Harriet's name nor her deeds are an integral part of the education of American youth.

This is not the place for detailed examination of the reasons for this suppression through historical omission. But it is pertinent to remark that in the revisionist theory of the origins of the American Civil War, economic and political forces are emphasized, and humanitarianism is accorded little causal significance. Consequently, those among the abolitionist leaders who cannot be categorized as self-seeking politicians or unrestrained fanatics are frequently omitted from the histories of the period. Yet there can be no real understanding or appreciation of the great drama played out on American soil a century ago without some recognition of the humanitarian "instincts" which motivated some of its principals. Harriet Tubman was exemplar *par excellence* of that humanitarian spirit. What better evidence of this does one need than the absence of bitterness over the government's persistent refusal to reward her for four years of service as occasional agent behind enemy lines, as scout for Union troops in the unfamiliar swamplands of the South, and as practical nurse in Union camp hospitals ministering to all—alike Yankee soldier, captured rebel, and fleeing slave. Through her we are re-introduced to many of those who like her were humanely inspired with no thought of earthly reward to work for the overthrow of slavery. Again we are made

aware of the penalties paid by some and the risks assumed
by all.

Though Harriet's birthdate is given as 1820 (or 1821)
two events occurring in 1793 mark the real beginnings of
her story. These were the perfection of the cotton gin and
the passage of the Fugitive Slave Law. The former vastly
increased the wealth potential of cotton farming and in
so doing increased the market value of slaves. The latter
established the legal right of recovery of run-away slaves
wherever found in the United States. By provision of this
law a slaveowner or his agent could arrest an alleged fugitive, haul him before a local magistrate, and if able to
convince that person of the validity of his claim, return
with the "run-away" to his home. In practical terms this
meant that every Negro, freeman or fugitive, ran the risk
of being impressed into slavery by the simple expedient of
having some white man appear and assert a claim of
ownership. The risk loses its remoteness when it is remembered that descriptions of run-away slaves tended to
be vague and general. Any Negro bearing a passing
resemblance to the alleged fugitive and unable immediately to produce documentary proof of his "free status"
was likely to be surrendered to the claimant white. Mrs.
Bradford has graphically described Harriet's determined
and successful effort to rescue one such victim of this
procedure. There were several other such incidents (not
all reported here) in the life of this forceful antagonist of
slavery.

While the records of the day do not permit us to say
with certainty whether or not many free Negroes were
impressed into slavery by these means the vigor with
which run-aways were sought, the alacrity with which
some magistrates acceded to the requests of slave owners,
plus the contemporary news reports of certain magisterial

hearings lead us to believe that the number was not insignificant. In an effort to reduce the number of such instances to a minimum and also as a means of forestalling the return of actual run-aways many of the Free States enacted Personal Liberty Laws. These generally required a more elaborate hearing as to the facts of the case (in some states a jury determination was required) before an alleged fugitive might be returned to his so-called owner. But it was the threat to the free Negro together with the shocking scenes of recovered runaways being marched through the streets of northern towns that made abolitionists like Sarah Bradford refer to the period prior to 1860 as "the years of terror of the Fugitive Slave Law."

For such leaders of the anti-slavery movement as Harriet Tubman, the Personal Liberty laws were never more than instruments of convenience to be used to delay and occasionally prevent the return of run-aways. Ultimate success for their program of subverting slavery by promoting effective escape required (1) a guaranteed haven for those who succeeded in escaping and (2) a reasonably safe escape route by which the fugitive could come to the place of safety. Once it became evident that our neighbor to the north would provide the haven, the terminus of the escape route was fixed and the underground railroad was born. But the path from plantation slave cabins to Canada was a circuitous one requiring many stop-overs. With only the North Star to guide them, escaping slaves might easily be apprehended by their owner-pursuers or fall prey to the wiles of professional slave chasers. What was needed were men and women familiar with the ways of the chase who were prepared to journey into the Southland, organize small bands of escapees and escort them from one stop-over point (called junctions) to the other in the long trek from plantation to Canada. Dubbed "conductors" these intrepid persons became the real heroes and heroines of the Underground Railroad. And of the many who served in this capacity none was more resourceful, more elusive, more eagerly hunted (rewards for her capture at one time totalled $40,000), or more successful than Harriet Tubman.

Mrs. Bradford does not tell us much about Harriet's life after her return to her home in Auburn (New York) following the close of the Civil War. But that too is a fascinating tale. This illiterate and penniless woman, now aged far beyond her years and suffering from frequent and prolonged periods of somnolence, immediately upon her return set about to save her home from mortgage foreclosure, to care for her own now very aged parents, and to urge the establishment of a home for the indigent aged Negroes of the community. When after several years of effort it appeared that insufficient funds would be raised to build such a home for the aged, Harriet cheerfully converted her own quarters to this purpose. Touched by her selflessness the people of Auburn rallied to her aid and established the Harriet Tubman Home for Aged and Indigent Negroes. After her death in 1913 a subscription campaign was launched to collect funds for a monument in the town square. The campaign was soon subscribed and the monument stands today in mute testimony to a woman of indomitable will—truly a Moses of Her People who having led them out of the land of Egypt, out of the House of Bondage and into the land of Canaan now sought to make meaningful the promise of freedom.

BUTLER A. JONES
Ohio Wesleyan University

HARRIET

The Moses of Her People

BY

SARAH H. BRADFORD

"Farewell, ole Marster, don't think hard of me,
I'm going on to Canada, where all de slaves are free."

"Jesus, Jesus will go wid you,
He will lead you to His throne,
He who died has gone before you,
Trod de wine-press all alone."

PREFACE.

THE title I have given my black heroine, in this second edition of her story, viz.: THE MOSES OF HER PEOPLE, may seem a little ambitious, considering that this Moses was a woman, and that she succeeded in piloting only three or four hundred slaves from the land of bondage to the land of freedom.

But I only give her here the name by which she was familiarly known, both at the North and the South, during the years of terror of the Fugitive Slave Law, and during our last Civil War, in both of which she took so prominent a part.

And though the results of her unexampled heroism were not to free a whole nation of bond-men and bond-women, yet this object was as much the desire of her heart, as it was of that of the great leader of Israel. Her cry to the slave-holders, was ever like his to Pharaoh, " Let my people go !" and

not even he imperiled life and limb more willingly, than did our courageous and self-sacrificing
friend.

Her name deserves to be handed down to pos-
terity, side by side with the names of Jeanne D'Arc,
Grace Darling, and Florence Nightingale, for not
one of these women, noble and brave as they were,
has shown more courage, and power of endurance,
in facing danger and death to relieve human suffering, than this poor black woman, whose story I
am endeavoring in a most imperfect way to give you.

Would that Mrs. Stowe had carried out the plan
she once projected, of being the historian of our
sable friend ; by her graphic pen, the incidents of
such a life might have been wrought up into a tale
of thrilling interest, equaling, if not exceeding her
world renowned " Uncle Tom's Cabin."

The work fell to humbler hands, and the first
edition of this story, under the title of " Harriet
Tubman," was written in the greatest possible
haste, while the writer was preparing for a voyage
to Europe.   There was pressing need for this
book, to save the poor woman's little home from
being sold under a mortgage, and letters and facts

were penned down rapidly, as they came in. The book has now been in part re-written and the letters and testimonials placed in an appendix.

For the satisfaction of the incredulous (and there will naturally be many such, when so strange a tale is repeated to them), I will here state that so far as it has been possible, I have received corroboration of every incident related to me by my heroic friend. I did this for the satisfaction of others, not for my own. No one can hear Harriet talk, and not believe every word she says. As Mr. Sanborn says of her, " she is too *real* a person, not to be true."

Many incidents quite as wonderful as those related in the story, I have rejected, because I had no way in finding the persons who could speak to their truth.

This woman was the friend of William H. Seward, of Gerritt Smith, of Wendell Phillips, of William Lloyd Garrison, and of many other distinguished philanthropists before the War, as of very many officers of the Union Army during the conflict.

After her almost superhuman efforts in making

her own escape from slavery, and then returning to the South *nineteen times,* and bringing away with her over three hundred fugitives, she was sent by Governor Andrew of Massachusetts to the South at the beginning of the War, to act as spy and scout for our armies, and to be employed as hospital nurse when needed.

Here for four years she labored without any remuneration, and during the time she was acting as nurse, never drew but twenty days' rations from our Government. She managed to support herself, as well as to take care of the suffering soldiers.

Secretary Seward exerted himself in every possible way to procure her a pension from Congress, but red-tape proved too strong even for him, and her case was rejected, because it did not come under any recognized law.

The first edition of this little story was published through the liberality of Gerritt Smith, Wendell Phillips, and prominent men in Auburn, and the object for which it was written was accomplished. But that book has long been out of print, and the facts stated there are all unknown to the present generation.

There have, I am told, often been calls for the book, which could not be answered, and I have been urged by many friends as well as by Harriet herself, to prepare another edition. For another necessity has arisen and she needs help again not for herself, but for certain helpless ones of her people. Her own sands are nearly run, but she hopes, 'ere she goes home, to see this work, a hospital, well under way. Her last breath and her last efforts will be spent in the cause of those for whom she has already risked so much.

For them her tears will fall,
For them her prayers ascend;
To them her toils and cares be given,
Till toils and cares shall end.

S. H. B.

Letter from Mr. Oliver Johnson for the second edition :

NEW YORK, *March* 6, 1886.

MY DEAR MADAM :

I am very glad to learn that you are about to publish a revised edition of your life of that heroic woman, Harriet Tubman, by whose assistance so many American slaves were enabled to break their bonds.

During the period of my official connection with the Anti-Slavery office in New York, I saw her frequently, when she came there with the companies of slaves, whom she had successfully piloted away from the South ; and oftened listened with wonder to the story of her adventures and hair-breadth escapes.

She always told her tale with a modesty which showed how unconscious she was of having done anything more than her simple duty. No one who listened to her could doubt her perfect truthfulness and integrity.

Her shrewdness in planning the escape of slaves, her skill in avoiding arrest, her courage in every emergency, and her willingness to endure hardship and face any danger for the sake of her poor followers was phenomenal.

I regret to hear that she is poor and ill, and hope the sale of your book will give her the relief she so much needs and so well deserves.

Yours truly,

OLIVER JOHNSON.

AUBURN THEOL. SEMINARY,
March 16, 1886.

BY PROFESSOR HOPKINS

The remarkable person who is the subject of the following sketch, has been residing mostly ever since the close of the war in the outskirts of the City of Auburn, during all which time I have been well acquainted with her. She has all the characteristics of the pure African race strongly marked upon her, though from which one of the various tribes that once fed the Barracoons, on the Guinea coast, she derived her indomitable courage and her passionate love of freedom I know not; perhaps from the Fellatas, in whom those traits were predominant.

Harriet lives upon a farm which the twelve hundred dollars given her by Mrs. Bradford from the proceeds of the first edition of this little book, enabled her to redeem from a mortgage held by the late Secretary Seward.

Her household is very likely to consist of several old black people, "bad with the rheumatize," some forlorn wandering woman, and a couple of small images of God cut in ebony. How she manages to feed and clothe herself and them, the Lord best knows. She has too much pride and too much faith to beg. She takes thankfully, but without any great effusiveness of gratitude, whatever God's messengers bring her.

I have never heard that she absolutely lacked. There are some good people in various parts of the country, into whose hearts God sends the thought, from time to time, that Harriet may be at the bottom of the flour sack, or of the potatoes, and the "help in time of need" comes to her.

Harriet's simplicity and ignorance have, in some cases, been imposed upon, very signally in one instance in Auburn, a few years ago; but nobody who knows her has the slightest doubt of her perfect integrity.

The following sketch taken by Mrs. Bradford, chiefly from Harriet's own recollections, which are wonderfully distinct and minute, but also from other corroborative sources, gives but a very imperfect account of what this woman has been.

Her color, and the servile condition in which she was born and reared, have doomed her to obscurity, but a more heroic soul did not breathe in the bosom of Judith or of Jeanne D'Arc.

No fear of the lash, the blood-hound, or the fiery stake, could divert her from her self-imposed task of leading as many as possible of her people "from the land of Egypt, from the house of bondage."

The book is good literature for the black race, or the white race, and though no similar conditions may arise, to test the possibilities that are in any of them, yet the example of this poor slave woman may well stand out before them, and before all people, black or white, to show what a lofty and martyr spirit may accomplish, struggling against overwhelming obstacles.

HARRIET,

THE MOSES OF HER PEOPLE.

ON a hot summer's day, perhaps sixty years ago, a group of merry little darkies were rolling and tumbling in the sand in front of the large house of a Southern planter. Their shining skins gleamed in the sun, as they rolled over each other in their play, and their voices, as they chattered together, or shouted in glee, reached even to the cabins of the negro quarter, where the old people groaned in spirit, as they thought of the future of those unconscious young revelers ; and their cry went up, "O, Lord, how long ! "

Apart from the rest of the children, on the top rail of a fence, holding tight on to the tall gate post, sat a little girl of perhaps thirteen years of age ; darker than any of the others, and with a more decided *woolliness* in the hair ; a pure unmiti-

gated African. She was not so entirely in a state
of nature as the rollers in the dust beneath her;
but her only garment was a short woolen skirt,
which was tied around her waist, and reached about
to her knees. She seemed a dazed and stupid child,
and as her head hung upon her breast, she looked
up with dull blood-shot eyes towards her young
brothers and sisters, without seeming to see them.
Bye and bye the eyes closed, and still clinging to
the post, she slept. The other children looked up
and said to each other, " Look at Hatt, she's done
gone off agin ! " Tired of their present play
ground they trooped off in another direction, but
the girl slept on heavily, never losing her hold on
the post, or her seat on her perch. Behold here,
in the stupid little negro girl, the future deliverer
of hundreds of her people ; the spy and scout of
the Union armies; the devoted hospital nurse; the
protector of hunted fugitives ; the eloquent speaker
in public meetings ; the cunning eluder of pursuing man-hunters ; the heaven guided pioneer
through dangers seen and unseen ; in short, as she
has well been called, " The Moses of her People."

Here in her thirteenth year she is just recovering

from the first terrible effects of an injury inflicted
by her master, who in an ungovernable fit of rage
threw a heavy weight at the unoffending child,
breaking in her skull, and causing a pressure upon
her brain, from which in her old age she is suffering still. This pressure it was which caused the
fits of somnolency so frequently to come upon her,
and which gave her the appearance of being stupid and half-witted in those early years. But that
brain which seemed so dull was full of busy
thoughts, and her life problem was already trying
to work itself out there.

She had heard the shrieks and cries of women
who were being flogged in the negro quarter ; she
had listened to the groaned out prayer, "Oh, Lord,
have mercy ! " She had already seen two older
sisters taken away as part of a chain gang, and
they had gone no one knew whither ; she had seen
the agonized expression on their faces as they
turned to take a last look at their "Old Cabin
Home ; " and had watched them from the top of
the fence, as they went off weeping and lamenting,
till they were hidden from her sight forever. She
saw the hopeless grief of the poor old mother, and

the silent despair of the aged father, and already she began to revolve in her mind the question, " Why should such things be? " " Is there no deliverance for my people? "

The sun shone on, and Harriet still slept seated on the fence rail. They, those others, had no anxious dreams of the future, and even the occasional sufferings of the present time caused them but a temporary grief. Plenty to eat, and warm sunshine to bask in, were enough to constitute their happiness ; Harriet, however, was not one of these. God had a great work for her to do in the world, and the discipline and hardship through which she passed in her early years, were only preparing her for her after life of adventure and trial ; and through these to come out as the Savior and Deliverer of her people, when she came to years of womanhood.

As yet she had seen no "visions," and heard no " voices ; " no foreshadowing of her life of toil and privation, of flight before human blood-hounds, of watchings, and hidings, of perils by land, and perils by sea, yea, and of perils by false brethren, or of miraculous deliverance had yet come to her. No hint of the great mission of her life, to guide her people from the land of bondage to the land of freedom. But, "Why should such things be?" and "Is there no help?" These were the questions of her waking hours.

The dilapidated state of things about the "Great House" told truly the story of waning fortunes, and poverty was pressing upon the master. One by one the able-bodied slaves disappeared; some were sold, others hired to other masters. No questions were asked; no information given; they simply disappeared. A "lady," for so she was designated, came driving up to the great house one day, to see if she could find there a young girl to take care of a baby. The lady wished to pay low wages, and so the most stupid and the most incapable of the children on the plantation was chosen to go with her. Harriet, who could command less wages than any other child of her age on the plantation, was therefore put into the wagon without a word of explanation, and driven off to the lady's house. It was not a very fine house, but Harriet had never before been in any dwelling better than the cabins of the negro quarter.

She was engaged as child's nurse, but she soon found that she was expected to be maid of all work by day, as well as child's nurse by night. The first task that was set her was that of sweeping and dusting a parlor. No information was vouchsafed as to the manner of going about this work, but she had often swept out the cabin, and this part of her task was successfully accomplished. Then at once she took the dusting cloth, and wiped off tables, chairs and mantel-piece. The dust, as dust will do, when it has nowhere else to go, at once settled again, and chairs and tables were soon covered with a white coating, telling a terrible tale against Harriet, when her Mistress came in to see how the work progressed. Reproaches, and savage words, fell upon the ears of the frightened child, and she was commanded to do the work all over again. It was done in precisely the same way, as before, with the same result. Then the whip was brought into requisition, and it was laid on with no light hand. Five times before breakfast this process was repeated, when a new actor appeared upon the scene. Miss Emily, a sister of the Mistress, had been roused from her morning slumber by the

sound of the whip, and the screams of the child ;
and being of a less imperious nature than her sister, she had come in to try to set matters right.

"Why do you whip the child, Susan, for not doing what she has never been taught to do ? Leave
her to me a few minutes, and you will see that she
will soon learn how to sweep and dust a room."
Then Miss Emily instructed the child to open the
windows, and sweep, then to leave the room, and
set the table, while the dust settled ; and after that
to return and wipe it off. There was no more
trouble of that kind. A few words might have set
the matter right before ; but in those days many a
poor slave suffered for the stupidity and obstinacy
of a master or mistress, more stupid than themselves.

When the labors, unremitted for a moment, of
the long day were over (for this mistress was an
economical woman, and intended to get the worth
of her money to the uttermost farthing), there was
still no rest for the weary child, for there was a
cross baby to be rocked continuously, lest it should
wake and disturb the mother's rest. The black
child sat beside the cradle of the white child, so

near the bed, that the lash of the whip would reach her if she ventured for a moment to forget her fatigues and sufferings in sleep. The Mistress reposed upon her bed with the whip on a little shelf over her head. People of color are, unfortunately, so constituted that even if the pressure of a broken skull does not cause a sleep like the sleep of the dead, the need of rest, and the refreshment of slumber after a day of toil, were often felt by them. No doubt, this was a great wrong to their masters, and a cheating them of time which belonged to them, but their slaves did not always look upon it in that light, and tired nature would demand her rights ; and so nature and the Mistress had a fight for it.

Rock, rock, went the cradle, and mother and child slept ; but alas ! the little black hand would sometimes slip down, and the head would droop, and a dream of home and mother would visit the weary one, only to be roughly dispelled by the swift descent of the stinging lash, for the baby had cried out and the mother had been awakened. This is no fictitious tale. That poor neck is even now covered with the scars which sixty years of life

have not been able to efface. It may be that she
was thus being prepared by the long habit of en-
forced wakefulness, for the night watches in the
woods, and in dens and caves of the earth, when the
pursuers were on her track, and the terrified ones
were trembling in her shadow. We do not thank
you for this, cruel woman ! for if you did her a service, you did it ignorantly, and only for your own
gratification. But Harriet's powers of endurance
failed at last, and she was returned to her master,
a poor, scarred wreck, nothing but skin and bone,
with the words that "She wasn't worth a six-
pence."

The poor old mother nursed her back to life,
and her naturally good constitution asserted itself,
so that as she grew older she began to show signs
of the wonderful strength which in after years,
when the fugitive slave law was in operation in
New York State, enabled her to seize a man from
the officers who had him in charge, and while
numbers were pursuing her, and the shot was flying like hail about her head, to bear him in her
own strong arms beyond the reach of danger.

As soon as she was strong enough for work,

Harriet was hired out to a man whose tyranny was worse, if possible, than that of the woman she had left. Now it was out of door drudgery which was put upon her. The labor of the horse and the ox, the lifting of barrels of flour and other heavy weights were given to her; and powerful men often stood astonished to see this woman perform feats of strength from which they shrunk incapable. This cruelty she looks upon as a blessing in disguise (a very questionable shape the blessing took, methinks), for by it she was prepared for after needs.

Still the pressure upon the brain continued, and with the weight half lifted, she would drop off into a state of insensibility, from which even the lash in the hand of a strong man could not rouse her. But if they had only known it, the touch of a gentle hand upon her shoulder, and her name spoken in tones of kindness, would have accomplished what cruelty failed to do.

The day's work must be accomplished, whether the head was racked with pain, and the frame was consumed by fever, or not ; but the day came at length when poor Harriet could work no more.

The sting of the lash had no power to rouse her now, and the new master finding her a dead weight on his hands, returned the useless piece of property to him who was called her "owner." And while she lay there helpless, this man was bringing other men to look at her, and offering her for sale at the lowest possible price ; at the same time setting forth her capabilities, if once she were strong and well again.

Harriet's religious character I have not yet touched upon. Brought up by parents possessed of strong faith in God, she had never known the time, I imagine, when she did not trust Him, and cling to Him, with an all-abiding confidence. She seemed ever to feel the Divine Presence near, and she talked with God "as a man talketh with his friend." Hers was not the religion of a morning and evening prayer at stated times, but when she felt a need, she simply told God of it, and trusted Him to set the matter right.

"And so," she said to me, "as I lay so sick on my bed, from Christmas till March, I was always praying for poor ole master. 'Pears like I didn't do nothing but pray for ole master. 'Oh, Lord, convert ole master;' 'Oh, dear Lord, change dat man's heart, and make him a Christian.' And all the time he was bringing men to look at me, and dey stood there saying what dey would give, and what dey would take, and all I could say was, 'Oh, Lord, convert ole master.' Den I heard dat as soon as I was able to move I was to be sent with my brudders, in the chain-gang to de far South. Then I changed my prayer, and I said, 'Lord, if you ain't never going to change dat man's heart, *kill him*, Lord, and take him out of de way, so he won't do no more mischief.' Next ting I heard ole master was dead ; and he died just as he had lived, a wicked, bad man. Oh, den it 'peared like I would give de world full of silver and gold, if I had it, to bring dat pore soul back, I would give *myself;* I would give eberyting ! But he was gone, I couldn't pray for him no more."

As she recovered from this long illness, a deeper religious spirit seemed to take possession of her than she had ever experienced before. She literally "prayed without ceasing." " 'Pears like, I prayed all de time," she said, "about my work, ebery-where ; I was always talking to de Lord. When

I went to the horse-trough to wash my face, and took up de water in my hands, I said, ' Oh, Lord, wash me, make me clean.' When I took up de towel to wipe my face and hands, I cried, ' Oh, Lord, for Jesus' sake, wipe away all my sins!' When I took up de broom and began to sweep, I groaned, ' Oh, Lord, whatsoebber sin dere be in my heart, sweep it out, Lord, clar and clean;' but I can't pray no more for pore ole master." No words can describe the pathos of her tones as she broke into these words of earnest supplication.

What was to become of the slaves on this plantation now that the master was dead? Were they all to be scattered and sent to different parts of the country? Harriet had many brothers and sisters, all of whom with the exception of the two, who had gone South with the chain-gang, were living on this plantation, or were hired out to planters not far away. The word passed through the cabins that another owner was coming in, and that none of the slaves were to be sold out of the State. This assurance satisfied the others, but it did not satisfy Harriet. Already the inward monitor was whispering to her, " Arise, flee for your life!" and in the visions of the night she saw the horsemen coming, and heard the shrieks of women and children, as they were being torn from each other, and hurried off no one knew whither. And beckoning hands were ever motioning her to come, and she seemed to see a line dividing the land of slavery from the land of freedom, and on the other side of that line she saw lovely white ladies waiting to welcome her, and to care for her. Already in her mind her people were the Israelites in the land of Egypt, while far away to the north *somewhere*, was the land of Canaan ; but had she as yet any prevision that *she* was to be the Moses who was to be their leader, through clouds of darkness and fear, and fires of tribulation to that promised land ? This she never said.

One day there were scared faces seen in the negro quarter, and hurried whispers passed from one to another. No one knew how it had come out, but some one had heard that Harriet and two of her brothers were very soon, perhaps to-day, perhaps to-morrow, to be sent far South with a gang, bought up for plantation work. Harriet was about twenty or twenty-five years old at this time, and the constantly recurring idea of escape at *sometime*, took sudden form that day, and with her usual promptitude of action she was ready to start at once.

She held a hurried consultation with her brothers, in which she so wrought upon their fears, that they expressed themselves as willing to start with her that very night, for that far North, where, could they reach it in safety, freedom awaited them. But she must first give some intimation of her purpose to the friends she was to leave behind, so that even if not understood at the time, it might be remembered afterward as her intended farewell. Slaves must not be seen talking together, and so it came about that their communication was often made by singing, and the words of their familiar hymns, telling of the heavenly journey, and the land of Canaan, while they did not attract the attention of the masters, conveyed to their brethren and sisters in bondage something more than met the ear. And so she sang, accompanying the words, when for a moment unwatched, with a meaning look to one and another:

" When dat ar ole chariot comes,
I'm gwine to lebe you,
I'm boun' for de promised land,
Frien's, I'm gwine to lebe you."

Again, as she passed the doors of the different cabins, she lifted up her well-known voice ; and many a dusky face appeared at door or window, with a wondering or scared expression ; and thus she continued:

" I'm sorry, frien's, to lebe you,
Farewell! oh, farewell !
But I'll meet you in de mornin',
Farewell! oh, farewell !

" I'll meet you in de mornin',
When you reach de promised land ;
On de oder side of Jordan,
For I'm boun' for de promised land."

The brothers started with her, but the way was strange, the north was far away, and all unknown, the masters would pursue and recapture them, and their fate would be worse than ever before; and so they broke away from her, and bidding her good-bye, they hastened back to the known horrors of slavery, and the dread of that which was worse.

Harriet was now left alone, but after watching the retreating forms of her brothers, she turned her face toward the north, and fixing her eyes on the guiding star, and committing her way unto the Lord, she started again upon her long, lonely journey. Her farewell song was long remembered in the cabins, and the old mother sat and wept for her lost child. No intimation had been given her of Harriet's intention, for the old woman was of a most impulsive disposition, and her cries and lamentations would have made known to all within hearing Harriet's intended escape. And so, with only the North Star for her guide, our heroine started on the way to liberty. "For," said she, "I had reasoned dis out in my mind; there was one of two things I had a *right* to, liberty, or death; if I could not have one, I would have de oder; for no man should take me alive; I should fight for my liberty as long as my strength lasted, and when de time came for me to go, de Lord would let dem take me."

And so without money, and without friends, she started on through unknown regions ; walking by night, hiding by day, but always conscious of an

invisible pillar of cloud by day, and of fire by
night, under the guidance of which she journeyed
or rested. Without knowing whom to trust, or
how near the pursuers might be, she carefully felt
her way, and by her native cunning, or by God
given wisdom, she managed to apply to the right
people for food, and sometimes for shelter;
though often her bed was only the cold ground,
and her watchers the stars of night.

After many long and weary days of travel, she
found that she had passed the magic line, which
then divided the land of bondage from the land of
freedom. But where were the lovely white ladies
whom in her visions she had seen, who, with arms
outstretched, welcomed her to their hearts and
homes. All these visions proved deceitful : she
was more alone than ever ; but she had crossed
the line ; no one could take her now, and she
would never call any man " Master " more.

"I looked at my hands," she said, "to see if I
was de same person now I was free. Dere was
such a glory ober eberything, de sun came like
gold trou de trees, and ober de fields, and I felt
like I was in heaven." But then came the bitter

drop in the cup of joy. She was alone, and her kindred were in slavery, and not one of them had the courage to dare what she had dared. Unless she made the effort to liberate them she would never see them more, or even know their fate.

"I knew of a man," she said, "who was sent to the State Prison for twenty-five years. All these years he was always thinking of his home, and counting by years, months, and days, the time till he should be free, and see his family and friends once more. The years roll on, the time of imprisonment is over, the man is free. He leaves the prison gates, he makes his way to his old home, but his old home is not there. The house in which he had dwelt in his childhood had been torn down, and a new one had been put up in its place ; his family were gone, their very name was forgotten, there was no one to take him by the hand to welcome him back to life."

"So it was wid me," said Harriet, "I had crossed de line of which I had so long been dreaming. I was free ; but dere was no one to welcome me to de land of freedom, I was a stranger in a strange land, and my home after all was

down in de old cabin quarter, wid de ole folks,
and my brudders and sisters. But to dis solemn
resolution I came ; I was free, and dey should be
free also; I would make a home for dem in de
North, and de Lord helping me, I would bring
dem all dere. Oh, how I prayed den, lying all
alone on de cold, damp ground ; " Oh, dear Lord,"
I said, " I haint got no friend but *you*. Come to
my help, Lord, for I'm in trouble ! "

It would be impossible here to give a detailed
account of the journeys and labors of this intrepid
woman for the redemption of her kindred and
friends, during the years that followed. Those
years were spent in work, almost by night and day,
with the one object of the rescue of her people
from slavery. All her wages were laid away with
this sole purpose, and as soon as a sufficient
amount was secured, she disappeared from her
Northern home, and as suddenly and mysteriously
she appeared some dark night at the door of one
of the cabins on a plantation, where a trembling
band of fugitives, forewarned as to time and place,
were anxiously awaiting their deliverer. Then she
piloted them North, traveling by night, hiding

by day, scaling the mountains, fording the rivers, threading the forests, lying concealed as the pursuers passed them. She, carrying the babies, drugged with paregoric, in a basket on her arm. So she went *nineteen* times, and so she brought away over three hundred pieces of living and breathing " property," with God given souls.

The way was so toilsome over the rugged mountain passes, that often the *men* who followed her would give out, and foot-sore, and bleeding, they would drop on the ground, groaning that they could not take another step. They would lie there and die, or if strength came back, they would return on their steps, and seek their old homes again. Then the revolver carried by this bold and daring pioneer, would come out, while pointing it at their heads she would say, " Dead niggers tell no tales ; you go on or die ! " And by this heroic treatment she compelled them to drag their weary limbs along on their northward journey.

But the pursuers were after them. A reward of $40,000 was offered by the slave-holders of the region from whence so many slaves had been spirited away, for the head of the woman who appeared so mysteriously, and enticed away their property, from under the very eyes of its owners. Our sagacious heroine has been in the car, having sent her frightened party round by some so-called "Under-ground Railway," and has heard this advertisement, which was posted over her head, read by others of the passengers. She never could read or write herself, but knowing that suspicion would be likely to fall upon any black woman traveling North, she would turn at the next station, and journey towards the South. Who would suspect a fugitive with such a price set upon her head, of rushing at railway speed into the jaws of destruction? With a daring almost heedless, she went even to the very village where she would be most likely to meet one of the masters to whom she had been hired; and having stopped at the Market and bought a pair of live fowls, she went along the street with her sun-bonnet well over her face, and with the bent and decrepit air of an aged woman. Suddenly on turning a corner, she spied her old master coming towards her. She pulled the string which tied the legs of the chickens; they began to flutter and scream, and as her master passed, she was stooping and busily engaged in attending to the fluttering fowls. And he went on his way, little thinking that he was brushing the very garments of the woman who had dared to steal herself, and others of his belongings.

At one time the pursuit was very close and vigorous. The woods were scoured in all directions, every house was visited, and every person stopped and questioned as to a band of black fugitives, known to be fleeing through that part of the country. Harriet had a large party with her then ; the children were sleeping the sound sleep that opium gives ; but all the others were on the alert, each one hidden behind his own tree, and silent as death. They had been long without food, and were nearly famished ; and as the pursuers seemed to have passed on, Harriet decided to make the attempt to reach a certain " station of the underground railroad " well known to her ; and procure food for her starving party. Under cover of the darkness, she started, leaving a cowering and trembling group in the woods, to whom a fluttering leaf, or a moving animal, were a sound of dread, bringing their hearts into their throats.

How long she is away! has she been caught and carried off, and if so what is to become of them? Hark ! there is a sound of singing in the distance, coming nearer and nearer.

And these are the words of the unseen singer, which I wish I could give you as I have so often heard them sung by herself :

> Hail, oh hail, ye happy spirits,
>   Death no more shall make you fear,
> Grief nor sorrow, pain nor anguish,
>   Shall no more distress you dere.
>
> Around Him are ten thousand angels,
>   Always ready to obey command;
> Dey are always hovering round you,
>   Till you reach de heavenly land.
>
> Jesus, Jesus will go wid you,
>   He will lead you to his throne;
> He who died, has gone before you,
>   Trod de wine-press all alone.
>
> He whose thunders shake creation,
>   He who bids de planets roll;
> He who rides upon the tempest,
>   And whose scepter sways de whole.

Dark and thorny is de pathway,
　　Where de pilgrim makes his ways;
But beyond dis vale of sorrow,
　　Lie de fields of endless days.

The air sung to these words was so wild, so full of plaintive minor strains, and unexpected quavers, that I would defy any white person to learn it, and often as I heard it, it was to me a constant surprise. Up and down the road she passes to see if the coast is clear, and then to make them certain that it is *their* leader who is coming, she breaks out into the plaintive strains of the song, forbidden to her people at the South, but which she and her followers delight to sing together :

Oh go down, Moses,
　　Way down into Egypt's land,
Tell old Pharaoh,
　　Let my people go.

Oh Pharaoh said he would go cross,
　　Let my people go,
And don't get lost in de wilderness.
　　Let my people go.

Oh go down, Moses,
  Way down into Egypt's land,
Tell old Pharaoh,
  Let my people go.

  You may hinder me here, but you can't up dere,
    Let my people go,
  He sits in de Hebben and answers prayer,
    Let my people go !

  Oh go down, Moses,
    Way down into Egypt's land,
  Tell old Pharaoh,
    Let my people go.

And then she enters the recesses of the wood, carrying hope and comfort to the anxious watchers there. One by one they steal out from their hiding places, and are fed and strengthened for another night's journey.

And so by night travel, by signals, by threatenings, by encouragement, through watchings and fastings, and I may say by direct interpositions of Providence, and miraculous deliverances, she brought her people to what was then their land of Canaan ; the State of New York. But alas ! this State did not continue to be their refuge. For in

1850, I think, the Fugitive Slave Law was put in force, which bound the people north of Mason and Dixon's line, to return to bondage any fugitive found in their territories.

"After that," said Harriet, "I wouldn't trust Uncle Sam wid my people no longer, but I brought 'em all clar off to Canada."

On her seventh or eighth journey, she brought with her a band of fugitives, among whom was a very remarkable man, whom I knew only by the name of "Joe." Joe was a noble specimen of a negro, enormously tall, and of splendid muscular development. He had been hired out by his master to another planter, for whom he had worked for six years, saving him all the expense of an overseer, and taking all trouble off from his hands. He was such a very valuable piece of property, and had become so absolutely necessary to the planter to whom he was hired, that he determined to buy him at any cost. His old master held him proportionately high. But by paying one thousand dollars down, and promising to pay another thousand in a certain time, the purchase was made, and this chattel passed over into the hands of a new owner.

The morning after the purchase was completed, the new master came riding down on a tall, powerful horse into the negro quarter, with a strong new rawhide in his hand, and stopping before Joe's cabin, called to him to come out. Joe was just eating his breakfast, but with ready obedience, he hastened out at the summons. Slave as he was, and accustomed to scenes of brutality, he was surprised when the order came, " Now, Joe, strip, and take a licking." Naturally enough, he demurred at first, and thought of resisting the order; but he called to mind a scene he had witnessed a few days before in the field, the particulars of which are too horrible to be given here, and he thought it the wisest course to submit; but first he tried a gentle remonstrance.

" Mas'r," said he, " habn't I always been faithful to you ? Habn't I worked through sun an' rain, early in de mornin' an' late at night; habn't I saved you an oberseer by doin' his work ? hab you anything to complain agin me ? "

" No, Joe, I have no complaint to make of you. You're a good nigger, an' you've always worked well. But you belong to *me* now; you're *my* nigger, and the first lesson my niggers have to learn is that I am master and they belong to me, and are never to resist anything I order them to do. So I always begin by giving them a good licking. Now strip and take it."

Joe saw that there was no help for him, and that for the time he must submit. He stripped off his clothing, and took his flogging without a word, but as he drew his shirt up over his torn and bleeding back, he said to himself: " Dis is de first an' de last." As soon as he was able he took a boat, and under cover of the night, rowed down the river, and made his way to the cabin of " Old Ben," Harriet's father, and said to him: " Nex' time *Moses* comes, let me know."

It was not long after this time, that the mysterious woman appeared—the woman on whom no one could lay his finger—and men, women, and children began to disappear from the plantations. One fine morning Joe was missing, and call as loud as he might, the master's voice had no power to bring him forth. Joe had certainly fled; and his brother William was gone, and Peter and Eliza. From other plantations other slaves were missing, and before their masters were awake to the fact, the party of fugitives, following their intrepid leader, were far on their way towards liberty.

The adventures of this escaping party would of themselves fill a volume. They hid in potato holes by day, while their pursuers passed within a few feet of them; they were passed along by friends in various disguises; they scattered and separated; some traveling by boat, some by wagons, some by cars, others on foot, to meet at some specified station of the under-ground railroad. They met at the house of Sam Green,* the man who was afterwards sent to prison for ten years for having a copy of " Uncle Tom's Cabin " in his house. And so, hunted and hiding and wandering, they found themselves at last at the entrance of the long

---

* In mentioning to me the circumstances of Sam Green's imprisonment, Harriet, who had no acquaintance with books, merely mentioned the fact as it had come to her own knowledge. But I have lately come across a book in the Astor Library which confirms the story precisely as she stated it.   It is in a book by Rev. John Dixon Long, of Philadelphia.   He says, " Samuel Green, a free colored man of Dorchester County, Maryland, was sentenced to ten years' confinement in the

bridge which crosses the river at Wilmington, Delaware.

No time had been lost in posting up advertisements and offering rewards for the capture of these fugitives; for Joe in particular the reward offered was very high. First a thousand dollars, then fifteen hundred, and then two thousand, "an' all expenses clar an' clean for his body in Easton Jail." This high reward stimulated the efforts of the officers who were usually on the lookout for escaping fugitives, and the added rewards for others of the party, and the high price set on Harriet's head, filled the woods and highways with eager hunters after human prey. When Harriet and her companions approached the long Wilmington Bridge, a warning was given them by some secret friend, that

---

Maryland State Prison, at the spring term of the County Court held in Cambridge, Md.

"What was the crime imputed to this man, born on American soil, a man of good moral character, a local preacher in the Methodist Episcopal Church; a husband and a father? Simply this: A copy of 'Uncle Tom's Cabin' *had been found in his possession.* It was not proved that he had ever read it to the colored people."

the advertisements were up, and the bridge was guarded by police officers. Quick as lightning the plans were formed in her ready brain, and the terrified party were separated and hidden in the houses of different friends, till her arrangements for their further journey were completed.

There was at that time residing in Wilmington an old Quaker, whom I may call *my* " friend," for though I never saw his face, I have had correspondence with him in reference to Harriet and her followers. This man, whose name was Thomas Garrett, and who was well known in those days to the friends of the slave, was a man of a wonderfully large and generous heart, through whose hands during those days of distress and horror, no less than three thousand self-emancipated men, women and children passed on their way to freedom. He gave heart, hand, and means to aid these poor fugitives, and to our brave Harriet he often rendered most efficient help in her journeys back and forth.

He was the proprietor of a very large shoe establishment ; and not one of these poor travelers ever left his house without a present of a new pair of shoes and other needed help. No sooner had this good man received intelligence of the condition of these poor creatures, than he devised a plan to elude the vigilance of the officers in pursuit, and bring Harriet and her party across the bridge. Two wagons filled with bricklayers were engaged, and sent over ; this was a common sight there, and caused no remark. They went across the bridge singing and shouting, and it was not an unexpected thing that they should return as they went. After nightfall (and, fortunately, the night was very dark) the same wagons recrossed the bridge, but with an unlooked-for addition to their party. The fugitives were lying close together on the bottom of the wagons ; the bricklayers were on the seats, still singing and shouting ; and so they passed the guards, who were all unsuspicious of the nature of the load contained in the wagons, or of the amount of property thus escaping their hands.

The good man, Thomas Garrett, who was in a very feeble state of health when he last wrote me, and has now gone to his reward, supplied them with all needed comforts, and sent them on their way refreshed, and with renewed courage. And

Harriet here set up her Ebenezer, saying, "Thus far hath the Lord helped me!" But many a danger, and many a fright, and many a deliverance awaited them, before they reached the city of New York. And even there they were not safe, for the Fugitive Slave Law was in operation, and their only refuge was Canada, which was now their promised land.

They finally reached New York in safety: and this goes almost without saying, for I may as well mention here that of the three hundred and more fugitives whom Harriet piloted from slavery, not one was ever recaptured, though all the cunning and skill of white men, backed by offered rewards of large sums of money, were brought into requisition for their recovery.

As they entered the anti-slavery office in New York, Mr. Oliver Johnson rose up and exclaimed, "Well, Joe, I am glad to see the man who is worth $2,000 to his master." At this Joe's heart sank. "Oh, Mas'r, how did you know me!" he panted. "Here is the advertisement in our office," said Mr. Johnson, "and the description is so close that no one could mistake it." And had he come through all these perils, had he traveled by day and night, and suffered cold and hunger, and lived in constant fear and dread, to find that far off here in New York State, he was recognized at once by the advertisement? How, then, was he ever to reach Canada? " And how far off is Canada?" he asked. He was shown the map of New York State, and the track of the railroad, for more than three hundred miles to Niagara, where he would cross the river, and be free. But the way seemed long and full of dangers. They were surely safer on their own tired feet, where they might hide in forests and ditches, and take refuge in the friendly underground stations ; but here, where this large party would be together in the cars, surely suspicion would fall upon them, and they would be seized and carried back. But Harriet encouraged him in her cheery way. He must not give up now. " De Lord had been with them in six troubles, and he would not desert them in de seventh." And there was nothing to do but to go on. As Moses spoke to the children of Israel, when compassed before and behind by dangers, so she spake to her people, that they should " go forward."

Up to this time, as they traveled they had talked and sung hymns together, like Pilgrim and his friends, and Joe's voice was the loudest and sweetest among them ; but now he hanged his harp upon the willows, and could sing the Lord's songs no more.

"From dat time," in Harriet's language, " Joe was silent ; he talked no more ; he sang no more ; he sat wid his head on his hand, an' nobody could 'rouse him, nor make him take any intrust in anything."

They passed along in safety through New York State, and at length found themselves approaching the Suspension Bridge. They could see the promised land on the other side. The uninviting plains of Canada seemed to them,

> " Sweet fields beyond the swelling flood,
>   All dressed in living green ; "

but they were not safe yet. Until they reached the center of the bridge, they were still in the power of their pursuers, who might at any pause enter the car, and armed with the power of the law, drag them back to slavery. The rest of the party

were happy and excited ; they were simple, ignorant creatures, and having implicit trust in their
leader, they felt safe when with her, and no immediate danger threatened them.   But Joe was of a
different mould.   He sat silent and sad, always
thinking of the horrors that awaited him if recaptured.   As it happened, all the other passengers
were people who sympathized with them, understanding them to be a band of fugitives, and they
listened with tears, as Harriet and all except poor
Joe lifted up their voices and sang :

> I'm on the way to Canada,
> > That cold and dreary land,
> De sad effects of slavery,
> > I can't no longer stand;
> I've served my Master all my days,
> > Widout a dime reward,
> And now I'm forced to run away,
> > To flee de lash, abroad;
> Farewell, ole Master, don't think hard of me,
> I'm traveling on to Canada, where all de slaves are free.

> De hounds are baying on my track,
> > Ole Master comes behind,
> Resolved that he will bring me back,
> > Before I cross the line;

I'm now embarked for yonder shore,
    Where a man's *a man* by law,
De iron horse will bear me o'er,
    To " shake de lion's paw ; "
Oh, righteous Father, wilt thou not pity me,
And help me on to Canada, where all de slaves are free.

Oh I heard Queen Victoria say,
    That if we would forsake,
Our native land of slavery,
    And come across de lake;
Dat she was standing on de shore,
    Wid arms extended wide,
To give us all a peaceful home,
    Beyond de rolling tide;
Farewell, ole Master, don't think hard of me,
I'm traveling on to Canada, where all de slaves are free.

No doubt the simple creatures with her expected
to cross a wide lake instead of a rapid river, and to
see Queen Victoria with her· crown upon her head,
waiting with arms extended wide, to fold them all
in her embrace. There was now but " one wide
river to cross," and the cars rolled on to the bridge.
In the distance was heard the roar of the mighty
cataract, and now as they neared the center of the
bridge, the falls might be clearly seen. Harriet

was anxious to have her companions see this wonderful sight, and succeeded in bringing all to the windows, except Joe. But Joe still sat with his head on his hands, and not even the wonders of Niagara could draw him from his melancholy musings. At length as Harriet knew by the rise of the center of the bridge, and the descent immediately after, the line of danger was passed ; she sprang across to Joe's side of the car, and shook him almost out of his seat, as she shouted, " Joe ! you've shook de lion's paw !" This was her phrase for having entered on the dominions of England. But Joe did not understand this figurative expression. Then she shook him again, and put it more plainly, " Joe, you're in Queen Victoria's dominions ! You're a free man ! "

Then Joe arose. His head went up, he raised his hands on high, and his eyes, streaming with tears, to heaven, and then he began to sing and shout :

" Glory to God and Jesus too,
One more soul got safe;
Oh, go and carry the news,
One more soul got safe."

"Joe, come and look at the falls!"
        "Glory to God and Jesus too,
        One more soul got safe."
"Joe! it's your last chance.   Come and see de falls!"
        "Glory to God and Jesus too,
        One more soul got safe."

And this was all the answer.   The train stopped
on the other side ; and the first feet to touch
British soil, after those of the conductor, were
those of poor Joe.

Loud roared the waters of Niagara, but louder
still ascended the Anthem of praise from the over-
flowing heart of the freeman.   And can we doubt
that the strain was taken up by angel voices
and echoed and re-echoed through the vaults of
heaven :

        Glory to God in the highest,
        Glory to God and Jesus too,
        For all these souls now safe.

"The white ladies and gentlemen gathered
round him," said Harriet, "till I couldn't see Joe
for the crowd, only I heard his voice singing,
'Glory to God and Jesus too,' louder than ever."
A sweet young lady reached over her fine cambric

handkerchief to him, and as Joe wiped the great tears off his face, he said, "Tank de Lord! dere's only one more journey for me now, and dat's to Hebben!" As we bid farewell to Joe here, I may as well say that Harriet saw him several times after that, a happy and industrious freeman in Canada.*

On one of her journeys to the North, as she was piloting a company of refugees, Harriet came, just as morning broke, to a town, where a colored man

---

* In my recent interview with Mr. Oliver Johnson he told me of an interesting incident in the life of the good man, Thomas Garrett.

He was tried twice for assisting in the escape of fugitive slaves, and was fined so heavily that everything he possessed was taken from him and sold to pay the fine. At the age of sixty he was left without a penny, but he went bravely to work, and in some measure regained his fortune; all the time aiding, in every way possible, all stray fugitives who applied to him for help.

Again he was arrested, tried, and heavily fined, and as the Judge of the United States Court pronounced the sentence, he said, in a solemn manner: "Garrett, let this be a lesson to you, not to interfere hereafter with the cause of justice, by helping off runaway negroes."

had lived whose house had been one of her stations of the under-ground, or unseen railroad. They reached the house, and leaving her party huddled together in the middle of the street, in a pouring rain, Harriet went to the door, and gave the peculiar rap which was her customary signal to her friends. There was not the usual ready response, and she was obliged to repeat the signal several times. At length a window was raised, and the head of a *white man* appeared, with the gruff question, "Who are you?" and "What do you want?" Harriet asked after her friend, and

---

The old man, who had stood to receive his sentence, here raised his head, and fixing his eyes on "the Court," he said :

"Judge—thee hasn't left me a dollar, but I wish to say to thee, and to all in this court room, that if anyone knows of a fugitive who wants a shelter, and a friend, *send him to Thomas Garrett*, and he will befriend him !"

Not Luther before the Council at Worms was grander than this brave old man in his unswerving adherence to principle. In those days that tried men's souls there were many men like this old Quaker, and many women too, who would have gone cheerfully to the fire and the stake, for the cause of suffering humanity ; men and women *these* " of whom the world was not worthy."

was told that he had been obliged to leave for "harboring niggers."

Here was an unforeseen trouble ; day was breaking, and daylight was the enemy of the hunted and flying fugitives. Their faithful leader stood one moment in the street, and in that moment she had flashed a message quicker than that of the telegraph to her unseen Protector, and the answer came as quickly ; in a suggestion to her of an almost forgotten place of refuge. Outside of the town there was a little island in a swamp, where the grass grew tall and rank, and where no human being could be suspected of seeking a hiding place. To this spot she conducted her party ; she waded the swamp, carrying in a basket two well-drugged babies (these were a pair of little twins, whom I have since seen well grown young women), and the rest of the company following. She ordered them to lie down in the tall, wet grass, and here she prayed again, and waited for deliverance. The poor creatures were all cold, and wet, and hungry, and Harriet did not dare to leave them to get supplies ; for no doubt the man at whose house she had knocked, had given the alarm in the

town ; and officers might be on the watch for
them. They were truly in a wretched condition,
but Harriet's faith never wavered, her silent prayer
still ascended, and she confidently expected help
from some quarter or other.

It was after dusk when a man came slowly walking along the solid pathway on the edge of the
swamp. He was clad in the garb of a Quaker ;
and proved to be a " friend " in need and indeed ;
he seemed to be talking to himself, but ears quick-
ened by sharp practice caught the words he was
saying :

" My wagon stands in the barn-yard of the next
farm across the way. The horse is in the stable ;
the harness hangs on a nail." And the man was
gone. Night fell, and Harriet stole forth to the
place designated. Not only a wagon, but a wagon
well provisioned stood in the yard ; and before
many minutes the party were rescued from their
wretched position, and were on their way rejoicing,
to the next town. Here dwelt a Quaker whom
Harriet knew, and he readily took charge of the
horse and wagon, and no doubt returned them to
their owner. How the good man who thus came

to their rescue had received any intimation of their being in the neighborhood Harriet never knew. But these sudden deliverances never seemed to strike her as at all strange or mysterious ; her prayer was the prayer of faith, and she *expected* an answer.

At one time, as she was on her way South for a party of slaves, she was stopped not far from the southern shore of the Chesapeake Bay, by a young woman, who had been for some days in hiding, and was anxiously watching for " Moses," who was soon expected to pass that way.

This girl was a young and pretty Mulatto, named Tilly, she had been lady's maid and dress-maker, for her Mistress. She was engaged to a young man from another plantation, but he had joined one of Harriet's parties, and gone North. Tilly was to have gone also at that time, but had found it impossible to get away. Now she had learned that it was her Master's intention to give her to a Negro of his own for his wife ; and in fear and desperation, she made a strike for free-dom. Friends had concealed her, and all had been on the watch for Moses.

The distress and excitement of the poor creature was so great, and she begged and implored in such agonized tones that Harriet would just see her safe to Baltimore, where she knew of friends who would harbor her, and help her on her way, that Harriet determined to turn about, and endeavor to take the poor girl thus far on her Northward journey.

They reached the shore of Chesapeake Bay too late to leave that night, and were obliged to hide for a night and day in the loft of an old out-house, where every sound caused poor Tilly to tremble as if she had an ague fit. When the time for the boat to leave arrived, a sad disappointment awaited them. The boat on which they had expected to leave was disabled, and another boat was to take its place. At that time, according to the law of Slavery, no Negro could leave his Master's land, or travel anywhere, without a pass, properly signed by his owner. Of course this poor fugitive had no pass; and Harriet's passes were her own wits; but among her many friends, there was one who seemed to have influence with the clerk of the boat, on which she expected to take

passage ; and she was the bearer of a note requesting, or commanding him to take these two women
to the end of his route, asking no questions.

Now here was an unforeseen difficulty ; the boat
was not going ; the clerk was not there ; all on the
other boat were strangers.   But forward they must
go, trusting in Providence.   As they walked down
to the boat, a gang of lazy white men standing
together, began to make comments on their appearance.

" Too many likely looking Niggers traveling
North, about these days."   " Wonder if these
wenches have got a pass."   " Where you going,
you two ? "   Tilly trembled and cowered, and
clung to her protector, but Harriet put on a bold
front, and holding the note given her by her friend
in her hand, and supporting her terrified charge,
she walked by the men, taking no notice of their
insults.

They joined the stream of people going up to get
their tickets, but when Harriet asked for hers, the
clerk eyed her suspiciously, and said : " You just
stand aside, you two; I'll attend to your case bye
and bye."

Harriet led the young girl to the bow of the boat, where they were alone, and here, having no other help, she, as was her custom, addressed herself to the Lord. Kneeling on the seat, and supporting her head on her hands, and fixing her eyes on the waters of the bay, she groaned:

" Oh, Lord ! You've been wid me in six troubles, *don't* desert me in the seventh !"

" Moses ! Moses !" cried Tilly, pulling her by the sleeve. " Do go and see if you can't get tickets now."

" Oh, Lord ! You've been wid me in six troubles, *don't* desert me in the seventh."

And so Harriet's story goes on in her peculiarly graphic manner, till at length in terror Tilly exclaimed:

" Oh, Moses ! the man is coming. What shall we do ?"

" Oh, Lord, you've been wid me in six troubles !"

Here the clerk touched her on the shoulder, and Tilly thought their time had come, but all he said was:

" You can come now and get your tickets," and their troubles were over.

What changed this man from his former suspicious and antagonistic aspect, Harriet never
knew. Of course she said it was " de Lord," but
as to the agency he used, she never troubled herself to inquire. She *expected* deliverance when she
prayed, unless the Lord had ordered otherwise,
and in that case she was perfectly willing to accept
the Divine decree.

When surprise was expressed at her courage
and daring, or at her unexpected deliverances, she
would always reply : " Don't, I tell you, Missus,
'twan't *me*, 'twas *de Lord!* Jes' so long as he
wanted to use me, he would take keer of me, an'
when he didn't want me no longer, I was ready
to go; I always tole him, I'm gwine to hole stiddy
on to you, an' you've got to see me trou."

There came a time when Harriet, who had already brought away as many of her family as she
could reach, besides all others who would trust
themselves to her care, became much troubled
in " spirit " about three of her brothers, having
had an intimation of some kind that danger was
impending over them. With her usual wonderful
cunning, she employed a friend to write a letter

for her to a man named Jacob Jackson, who lived near the plantation where these brothers were at that time the hired slaves.

Jacob Jackson was a free negro, who could both read and write, and who was under suspicion just then of having a hand in the disappearance of colored "property." It was necessary, therefore, to exercise great caution in writing to him, on his own account as well as that of the writer, and those whom she wished to aid. Jacob had an adopted son, William Henry Jackson, also free, who had come North. Harriet determined to sign her letter with William Henry's name, feeling sure that Jacob would be clever enough to understand by her peculiar phraseology, the meaning she intended to convey.

Therefore, after speaking of indifferent matters, the letter went on : " Read my letter to the old folks, and give my love to them, and tell my brothers to be always *watching unto prayer*, and when *the good old ship of Zion comes along, to be ready to step on board*." This letter was signed " William Henry Jackson."

Jacob was not allowed to have his letters in

those days, until the self-elected inspectors of correspondence had had the perusal of them, and
consulted over their secret meaning. These wise-
acres therefore assembled, wiped their glasses
carefully, put them on, and proceeded to examine
this suspicious document. What it meant they
could not imagine. William Henry Jackson had
no parents, or brothers, and the letter was incom-
prehensible. Study as they might, no light dawned
upon them, but their suspicions became stronger,
and they were sure the letter meant mischief.

White genius having exhausted itself, black
genius was brought into requisition. Jacob was
sent for, and the letter was placed in his hands.
He read between the lines, and comprehended
the hidden meaning at once. " Moses " had dic-
tated this letter, and Moses was coming. The
brothers must be on the watch, and ready to join
her at a moment's warning. But Moses must
hurry, for the word had gone forth that the
brothers were to be sent South, and the chain-
gang was being collected.

Jacob read the letter slowly, threw it down,
and said : " Dat letter can't be meant for me

no how; I can't make head or tail of it." And he walked off and took immediate measures to let Harriet's brothers know that she was on the way, and they must be ready at the given signal to start for the North.

It was the day before Christmas when Harriet arrived, and the brothers were to have started on the day after Christmas for the South. They started on Christmas-day, but with their faces turned in another direction, and instead of the chain-gang and the whip, they had the North Star for their guide, and the Moses of her people for their leader.

As usual, this mysterious woman appeared suddenly, and word was conveyed to the brothers that they were to be at Old Ben's cabin on Saturday night, ready to start. "Old Ben" was their father, and as the parents were not of much use now, Harriet was pretty certain that they would not be sent away, and so she left them till she had rescued the younger and more valuable members of the family.

Quite a number had assembled at the cabin when the hour came for starting, but one brother was missing. Something had detained John ; but when the time for starting had struck, Harriet's word was "forward," and she "nebber waited for no one."

Poor John was ready to start from his cabin in the negro quarter when his wife was taken ill, and in an hour or two another little heir to the blessings of slavery had come into the world.

John must go off for a "Granny," and being a faithful, affectionate creature, he could not leave his wife under the present circumstances.

After the birth of the child he determined to start. The North and freedom, or the South and life-long slavery, were the alternatives before him ; and this was his last chance. If he once reached the North, he hoped with the help of Moses to bring his wife and children there.

Again and again he tried to start out of the door, but a watchful eye was on him, and he was always arrested by the question, "Where you gwine, John ?" His wife had not been informed of the danger hanging over his head, but she knew he was uneasy, and she feared he was meditating a plan of escape. John told her he was going to try to get hired out on Christmas to another man, as that was the day on which such changes were made.

He left the house but stood near the window listening. He heard his wife sobbing and moaning, and not being able to endure it he went back to her. " Oh, John ! " she cried, " you's gwine to lebe me ! I know it ! but wherebber you go, John, don't forgit me an' de little children."

John assured her that wherever he went she should come. He might not come for her, but he would send Moses, and then he hurried away. He had many miles to walk to his old father's cabin, where he knew the others would be waiting for him, and at daybreak he overtook them in the " fodder house," not far from the home of the old people.

At that time Harriet had not seen her mother for six years, but she did not dare to let her know that four of her children were so near her on their way to the North, for she would have raised such an uproar in her efforts to detain them, that the whole neighborhood would have been aroused.

The poor old woman had been expecting her

sons to spend Christmas with her as usual. She had been hard at work in preparation for their arrival. The fatted pig had been killed, and had been converted into every form possible to the flesh of swine ; pork, bacon and sausages were ready, but the boys did not come, and there she sat watching and waiting.

In the night when Harriet with two of her brothers, and two other fugitives who had joined them arrived at the "fodder house," they were exhausted and well-nigh famished. They sent the two strange men up to the cabin to try to rouse "Old Ben," but not to let their mother know that her children were so near her.

The men succeeded in rousing Old Ben, who came out quietly, and as soon as he heard their story, went back into the house, gathered together a quantity of provisions, and came down to the fodder house. He placed the provisions inside the door, saying a few words of welcome to his children, but taking care *not to see them.* "I know what'll come of dis," he said, "an' I ain't gwine to see my chillen, no how." The close espionage under which these poor creatures dwelt, engendered in them a cunning and artifice, which to them seemed only a fair and right attempt on their part, to cope with power and cruelty constantly in force against them.

Up among the ears of corn lay the old man's children, and one of them he had not seen for six years. It rained in torrents all that Sunday, and there they lay among the corn, for they could not start till night. At about daybreak John had joined them. There were wide chinks in the boards of the fodder house, and through these they could see the cabin of the old folks, now quite alone in their old age. All day long, every few minutes, they would see the old woman come out, and shading her eyes with her hand, take a long look down the road to see if "de boys" were coming, and then with a sad and disappointed air she would turn back into the cabin, and they could almost hear her sigh as she did so.

What had become of the boys? Had they been sold off down South? Had they tried to escape and been retaken? Would she never see them or hear of them more?

I have often heard it said by Southern people

that "niggers had no feeling; they did not care when their children were taken from them." I have seen enough of them to know that their love for their offspring is quite equal to that of the "superior race," and it is enough to hear the tale of Harriet's endurance and self-sacrifice to rescue her brothers and sisters, to convince one that a heart, truer and more loving than that of many a white woman, dwelt in her bosom. I am quite willing to acknowledge that she was almost an anomaly among her people, but I have known many of her family, and so far as I can judge they all seem to be peculiarly intelligent, upright and religious people, and to have a strong feeling of family affection. There may be many among the colored race like them; certainly all should not be judged by the idle, miserable darkies who have swarmed about Washington and other cities since the War.

Two or three times while the group of fugitives were concealed in this loft of the fodder house, the old man came down and pushed food inside the door, and after nightfall he came again to accompany his children as far as he dared, upon their journey. When he reached the fodder house, he tied a handkerchief tight about his eyes, and one of his sons taking him by one arm, and Harriet taking him by the other, they went on their way talking in low tones together, asking and answering questions as to relatives and friends.

The time of parting came, and they bade him farewell, and left him standing in the middle of the road. When he could no longer hear their footsteps he turned back, and taking the handkerchief from his eyes, he hastened home.

But before Harriet and her brothers left, they had gone up to the cabin during the evening to take a silent farewell of the poor old mother. Through the little window of the cabin they saw her sitting by the fire, her head on her hand, rocking back and forth, as was her way when she was in great trouble; praying, no doubt, and wondering what had become of her children, and what new evil had befallen them.

With streaming eyes, they watched her for ten or fifteen minutes; but time was precious, and they must reach their next under-ground station before daylight, and so they turned sadly away.

When Christmas was over, and the men had not

returned, there began to be no small stir in the plantation from which they had escaped. The first place to search, of course, was the home of the old people. At the " Big House " nothing had been seen of them. The master said " they had generally come up there to see the house servants, when they came for Christmas, but this time they hadn't been round at all. Better go down to Old Ben's, and ask him."

They went to Old Ben's. No one was at home but " Old Rit," the mother. She said " not one of 'em came dis Christmas. She was looking for 'em all day, an' her heart was mos' broke about 'em."

Old Ben was found and questioned about his sons. Old Ben said, " He hadn't *seen one* of 'em dis Christmas." With all his deep religious feeling, Old Ben thought that in such a case as this, it was enough for him to keep to the *letter*, and let the man hunters find his sons if they could. Old Ben knew the Old Testament stories well. Perhaps he thought of Rahab who hid the spies, and received a commendation for it. Perhaps of Jacob and Abraham, and some of their rather questionable proceedings. He knew the New Testament also, but

I think perhaps he thought the kind and loving Saviour would have said to him, " Neither do I condemn thee." I doubt if he had read Mrs. Opie, and I wonder what judgment that excellent woman would have given in a case like this.

These poor fugitives, hunted like partridges upon the mountains, or like the timid fox by the eager sportsman, were obliged in self-defense to meet cunning with cunning, and to borrow from the birds and animals their mode of eluding their pursuers by any device which in the exigency of the case might present itself to them. They had a creed of their own, and a code of morals which we dare not criticise till we find our own lives and those of our dear ones similarly imperiled.

One of Harriet's other brothers had long been attached to a pretty mulatto girl named Catherine, who was owned by another master; but this man had other views for her, and would not let her marry William Henry. On one of Harriet's journeys this brother had made up his mind to make one of her next party to the North, and that Catherine should go also. He went to a tailor's and bought a new suit of clothes for a small person, and concealed them inside the fence of the garden of Catherine's master. This garden ran down to the bank of a little stream, and Catherine had been notified where to find the clothes. When the time came to get ready, Catherine boldly walked down to the foot of the garden, took up the bundle, and hiding under the bank, she put on the man's garments and sent her own floating down the stream.

She was soon missed, and all the girls in the house were set to looking for Catherine. Presently they saw coming up from the river a well-dressed little darkey boy, and they all ceased looking for Catherine, and stared at him. He walked directly by them, round the house, and out of the gate, without the slightest suspicion being excited as to who he was. In a few weeks from that time, this party were all safe in Canada.

William Henry died in Canada, but I have seen and talked with Catherine at Harriet's house.

I am not quite certain which company it was that was under her guidance on their Northward way, but at one time when a number of men were following her, she received one of her sudden intimations that danger was ahead. "Chillen," she

said, " we must stop here and cross dis ribber."
They were on the bank of a stream of some width,
and apparently a deep and rapid one. The men
were afraid to cross; there was no bridge and no
boat; but like her great pattern, she went forward
into the waters, and the men not knowing what else
to do, followed, but with fear and trembling. The
stream did not divide to make a way for them to
cross over, but to her was literally fulfilled the
promise :

"When through the deep waters I cause thee to go,
    The rivers of sorrow shall not overflow."

"For," said she, "Missus, de water never came
above my chin ; when we thought surely we were
all going under, it became shallower and shallower,
and we came out safe on the odder side." Then
there was another stream to cross, which was also
passed in safety. They found afterward that a
few rods ahead of them the advertisement of these
escaping fugitives was posted up, and the officers,
forewarned of their coming, were waiting for them.
But though the Lord thus marvelously protected
her from capture, she did not always escape the

consequences of exposure like this. It was in March that this passage of the streams was effected, and the weather was raw and cold; Harriet traveled a long distance in her wet clothing, and was afterward very ill for a long time with a very severe cold. I have often heard her tell this story; but some of the incidents, particularly that of her illness, were not mentioned by herself, but were written me by friend Garrett.

I hardly know how to approach the subject of the spiritual experiences of my sable heroine. They seem so to enter into the realm of the supernatural, that I can hardly wonder that those who never knew her are ready to throw discredit upon the story. Ridicule has been cast upon the whole tale of her adventures by the advocates of human slavery; and perhaps by those who would tell with awe-struck countenance some tale of ghostly visitation, or spiritual manifestation, at a dimly lighted "*seance.*"

Had I not known so well her deeply religious character, and her conscientious veracity, and had I not since the war, and when she was an inmate of my own house, seen such remarkable instances of what seemed to be her direct intercourse with heaven, I should not dare to risk my own character for veracity by making these things public in this manner.

But when I add that I have the strongest testimonials to her character for integrity from William H. Seward, Gerritt Smith, Wendell Phillips, Fred. Douglass, and my brother, Prof. S. M. Hopkins, who has known her for many years, I do not fear to brave the incredulity of any reader.

Governor Seward wrote of her :

" I have known Harriet long, and a nobler, higher spirit, or a truer, seldom dwells in human form."

Gerritt Smith, the distinguished philanthropist, was so kind as to write me expressing his gratification that I had undertaken this work, and added :

" I have often listened to Harriet with delight· on her visits to my family, and I am convinced that she is not only truthful, but that she has a rare discernment, and a deep and sublime philanthropy."

Wendell Phillips wrote me, mentioning that in Boston, Harriet earned the confidence and admira-

tion of all those who were working for freedom ;
and speaking of her labors during the war, he
added : " In my opinion there are few captains,
perhaps few colonels, who have done more for the
loyal cause since the war began, and few men who
did more before that time, for the colored race,
than our fearless and sagacious friend."

Many other letters I received; from Mr. Sanborn,
Secretary of the Massachusetts Board of Charities,
from Fred. Douglass, from Rev. Henry Fowler,
and from Union officers at the South during the
war, all speaking in the highest praise and admiration of the character and labors of my black
heroine.

Many of her passes also were sent me ; in which
she is spoken of as " Moses," for by that name she
was universally known. For the story of her heroic
deeds had gone before her, and the testimony of
all who knew her accorded with the words of Mr.
Seward :

" The cause of freedom owes her much ; the
country owes her much." And yet the country
was not willing to pay her anything. Mr. Seward's
efforts, seconded by other distinguished men, to

get a pension for her, were sneered at in Congress as absurd and quixotic, and the effort failed.

Secretary Seward, from whom Harriet purchased her little place near Auburn, died. The place had been mortgaged when this noble woman left her home, and threw herself into the work needed for the Union cause ; the mortgage was to be foreclosed. The old parents, then nearly approaching their centennial year, were to be turned out to die in a poor-house, when the sudden determination was taken to send out a little sketch of her life to the benevolent public, in the hope of redeeming the little home. This object, through the kindness of friends, was accomplished. The old people died in Harriet's own home, breathing blessings upon her for her devotion to them.

Now another necessity has arisen, and our sable friend, who never has been known to beg for herself, asks once more for help in accomplishing a favorite project for the good of her people. This, as she says, is "her last work, and she only prays de Lord to let her live till it is well started, and den she is ready to go." This work is the building of a hospital for old and disabled colored people ;

and in this she has already had the sympathy and aid of the good people of Auburn ; the mayor and his noble wife having given her great assistance in the meetings she has held in aid of this object. It is partly to aid her in this work, on which she has so set her heart, that this story of her life and labors is being re-written.

At one time, when she felt called upon to go down for some company of slaves, she was, as she knew, watched for everywhere (for there had been an excited meeting of slave-holders, and they were determined to catch her, dead or alive), her friends gathered round her, imploring her not to go on in the face of danger and death, for they were sure she would never be allowed to return. And this was her answer :

" Now look yer ! John saw de City, didn't he ? " " Yes, John saw de City." " Well, what did he see ? He saw twelve gates, didn't he ? Three of dose gates was on de north ; three of 'em was on de east ; an' three of 'em was on de west ; but dere was three more, an' dem was on de *south ;* an' I reckon, if dey kill me down dere, I'll git into one of dem gates, don't you ? "

Whether Harriet's ideas of the geographical bearings of the gates of the Celestial City as seen in the apocalyptic vision, were correct or not, we cannot doubt that she was right in the deduction her faith drew from them ; and that somewhere, whether North, East, South, or West, to our dim vision, there is a gate that will be opened for our good Harriet, where the welcome will be given, "Come in, thou blessed of my Father."

It is a peculiarity of Harriet, that she had seldom been known to intimate a wish that anything should be given to herself ; but when her people are in need, no scruples of delicacy stand in the way of her petitions, nay, almost her *demands* for help.

When, after rescuing so many others, and all of her brothers and sisters that could be reached, with their children, she received an intimation in some mysterious or supernatural way, that the old people were in trouble and needed her, she asked the Lord where she should go for the money to enable her to go for them. She was in some way, as she supposed, directed to the office of a certain gentleman, a friend of the slaves, in New York.

When she left the house of the friends with whom she was staying, she said : " I'm gwine to Mr. ————'s office, an' I ain't gwine to lebe dere, an' I ain't gwine to eat or drink, till I get money enough to take me down after de ole people."

She went into this gentleman's office.

" How do you do, Harriet? What do you want ? " was the first greeting.

" I want some money, sir."

" *You do !* How much do you want ? "

" I want twenty dollars, sir ! "

" *Twenty dollars !* Who told you to come here for twenty dollars ! "

" De Lord tole me, sir."

" He did; well I guess the Lord's mistaken this time."

" No, sir; de Lord's nebber mistaken ! Anyhow I'm gwine to sit here till I get it."

So she sat down and went to sleep. All the morning, and all the afternoon, she sat there still ; sometimes sleeping, sometimes rousing up, often finding the office full of gentlemen ; sometimes finding herself alone.

Many fugitives were passing through New York at this time, and those who came in supposed her to be one of them, tired out, and resting. Sometimes she would be roused up with the words:

"Come, Harriet! You had better go; there's no money for you here."

"No, sir; I'm not gwine to stir from here till I git my twenty dollars!"

She does not know all that happened, for deep sleep fell upon her; probably one of the turns of somnolency to which she has always been subject; but without doubt her story was whispered from one to another, and as her name and exploits were well known to many persons, the sympathies of some of those visitors to the office were aroused; at all events she came to full consciousness, at last, to find herself the happy possessor of *sixty dollars*, the contribution of these strangers. She went on her way rejoicing to bring her old parents from the land of bondage.

When she reached their home, she found that her old father was to be tried the next Monday for helping off slaves. And so, as she says in her forcible language, "I just removed my father's trial to a higher court, and brought him off to Canada."

The manner of their escape is detailed in the following letter from friend Garrett:

WILMINGTON, 6th Mo., 1868.

MY FRIEND: Thy favor of the 12th reached me yesterday, requesting such reminiscences as I could give respecting the remarkable labors of Harriet Tubman, in aiding her colored friends from bondage. I may begin by saying, living as I have in a slave State, and the laws being very severe where any proof could be made of any one aiding slaves on their way to freedom, I have not felt at liberty to keep any written word of Harriet's or my own labors, except in numbering those whom I have aided. For that reason I cannot furnish so interesting an account of Harriet's labors as I otherwise could, and now would be glad to do ; for in truth I never met with any person, of any color, who had more confidence in the voice of God, as spoken direct to her soul. She has frequently told me that she talked with God, and he talked with her every day of her life, and she has declared to me that she felt no more fear of being arrested by her former master, or any other person, when in his immediate neighborhood, than she did in the State of New York, or Canada, for she said she never ventured only where God sent her, and her faith in the Supreme Power truly was great.

I have now been confined to my room with indisposition more than four weeks, and cannot sit to write much ; but I feel so much interested in Harriet, that I will try to give some of the most remarkable incidents that now present themselves to my mind. The date of the commencement of her labors, I cannot certainly give ; but I think it must have been about 1845 ; from that time till 1860, I think she must have brought from the neighborhood where she had been held as a slave. from 60 to 80 persons,* from Maryland, some 80 miles from here. No slave who placed himself under her care, was ever arrested that I have heard of ; she mostly had her regular stopping places on her route ; but in one instance, when she had several stout men with her, some 30 miles below here, she said that God told her to stop, which she did ; and then asked him what she must

do. He told her to leave the road, and turn to the
left ; she obeyed, and soon came to a small stream
of tide water ; there was no boat, no bridge ; she
again inquired of her Guide what she was to do.
She was told to go through. It was cold, in the
month of March ; but having confidence in her
Guide, she went in ; the water came up to her
armpits ; the men refused to follow till they saw
her safe on the opposite shore. They then followed, and, if I mistake not, she had soon to wade
a second stream ; soon after which she came to a
cabin of colored people, who took them all in, put
them to bed, and dried their clothes, ready to proceed next night on their journey. Harriet had
run out of money, and gave them some of her
underclothing to pay for their kindness. When
she called on me two days after, she was so hoarse
she could hardly speak, and was also suffering with
violent toothache. The strange part of the story
we found to be, that the masters of these men
had put up the previous day, at the railroad station near where she left, an advertisement for
them, offering a large reward for their apprehen-
sion ; but they made a safe exit. She at one time

brought as many as seven or eight, several of whom were women and children. She was well known here in Chester County and Philadelphia, and respected by all true abolitionists. I had been in the habit of furnishing her and those who accompanied her, as she returned from her acts of mercy, with new shoes ; and on one occasion when I had not seen her for three months, she came into my store. I said, " Harriet, I am glad to see thee! I suppose thee wants a pair of new shoes." Her reply was, " I want more than that." I, in jest, said, " I have always been liberal with thee, and wish to be; but I am not rich, and cannot afford to give much." Her reply was : "God tells me you have money for me." I asked her "if God never deceived her ? " She said, " No ! " " Well ! how much does thee want ? " After studying a moment, she said : " About twenty-three dollars." I then gave her twenty-four dollars and some odd cents, the net proceeds of five pounds sterling, received through Eliza Wigham, of Scotland, for her. I had given some accounts of Harriet's labor to the Anti-Slavery Society of Edinburgh, of which Eliza Wigham was Secretary. On the read-

ing of my letter, a gentleman present said he would
send Harriet four pounds if he knew of any way to
get it to her. Eliza Wigham offered to forward it
to me for her, and that was the first money ever
received by me for her. Some twelve months
after, she called on me again, and said that God
told her I had some money for her, but not so
much as before. I had, a few days previous,
received the net proceeds of one pound ten shil-
lings from Europe for her. To say the least there
was something remarkable in these facts, whether
clairvoyance, or the divine impression on her mind
from the source of all power, I cannot tell ; but
certain it was she had a guide within herself other
than the written word, for she never had any education. She brought away her aged parents in a
singular manner. They started with an old horse,
fitted out in primitive style with a *straw collar*, a
pair of old chaise wheels, with a board on the axle
to sit on, another board swung with ropes, fastened
to the axle, to rest their feet on. She got her parents, who were both slaves belonging to different
masters, on this rude vehicle to the railroad, put
them in the cars, turned Jehu herself, and drove to

town in a style that no human being ever did before or since ; but she was happy at having arrived
safe. Next day, I furnished her with money to
take them all to Canada. I afterward sold their
horse, and sent them the balance of the proceeds.
I believe that Harriet succeeded in freeing all her
relatives but one sister and her three children.
Etc., etc.   Thy friend,

                                        THOS. GARRETT.

* Friend Garrett probably refers here to those who
passed through his hands. Harriet was obliged to
come by many different routes on her different
journeys, and though she never counted those
whom she brought away with her, it would seem,
by the computation of others, that there must have
been somewhat over three hundred brought by her
to the Northern States and Canada.

As I have before stated, with all Harriet's reluc-
tance to ask for anything for herself, no matter
how great her needs may be, no such scruples
trouble her if any of her people are in need. She
never hesitates to call upon her kind friends in
Auburn and in other places for help when her peo-

ple are in want. At one time, when some such
emergency had arisen, she went to see her friend,
Governor Seward, and boldly presented her case to
him.

" Harriet," he said, " you have worked for others
long enough. If you would ever ask anything for
yourself, I would gladly give it to you, but I will
not help you to rob yourself for others any
longer."

In spite of this apparent roughness, we may be
sure Harriet did not leave this noble man's house
empty handed.

And here I am reminded of a touching little
circumstance that occurred at the funeral of Secretary Seward.

The great man lay in his coffin. Friends, children, and admirers were gathered there. Everything that love and wealth could do had been
done ; around him were floral emblems of every
possible shape and design, that human ingenuity
could suggest, or money could purchase. Just before the coffin was to be closed, a woman black as
night stole quietly in, and laying a wreath of field
flowers *on his feet*, as quietly glided out again.

This was the simple tribute of our sable friend, and her last token of love and gratitude to her kind benefactor. I think he would have said, " This woman hath done more than ye all."

While preparing this second edition of Harriet's story, I have been much pleased to find that that good man, Oliver Johnson, is still living and in New York City. And I have just returned from a very pleasant interview with him. He remembers Harriet with great pleasure, though he has not seen her for many years. He speaks, as all who knew her do, of his entire confidence in her truthfulness and in the perfect integrity of her character.

He remembered her coming into his office with Joe, as I have stated it, and said he wished he could recall to me other incidents connected with her. But during those years, there were such numbers of fugitive slaves coming into the Anti-Slavery Office, that he might not tell the incidents of any one group correctly. No records were kept, as that would be so unsafe for the poor creatures, and those who aided them. He said, " You know Harriet never spoke of anything she had done, as if it was at all remarkable, or as if it deserved any commendation, but I remember one day, when she came into the office there was a Boston lady there, a warm-hearted, impulsive woman, who was engaged heart and hand in the Anti-Slavery cause.

Harriet was telling, in her simple way, the story of her last journey. A party of fugitives were to meet her in a wood, that she might conduct them North. For some unexplained reason they did not come. Night came on and with it a blinding snow storm and a raging wind. She protected herself behind a tree as well as she could, and remained all night alone exposed to the fury of the storm.

"Why, Harriet!" said this lady, "didn't you almost feel when you were lying alone, as if there was *no God?*" "Oh, no! missus," said Harriet, looking up in her child-like, simple way, "I jest asked Jesus to take keer of me, an' He never let me git *frost-bitten* one bit."

In 1860 the first gun was fired from Fort Sumter; and this was the signal for a rush to arms at the North and the South, and the war of the rebellion was begun. Troops were hurried off from the North to the West and the South, and battles raged in every part of the Southern States. By land and by sea, and on the Southern rivers, the conflict raged, and thousands and thousands of brave men shed their blood for what was maintained by each side to be the true principle.

This war our brave heroine had expected, and its result, the emancipation of the slaves. Three years before, while staying with the Rev. Henry Highland Garnet in New York, a vision came to her in the night of the emancipation of her people. Whether a dream, or one of those glimpses into the future, which sometimes seem to have been granted to her, no one can say, but the effect upon her was very remarkable.

She rose singing, "*My people are free!*" "*My people are free!*" She came down to breakfast singing the words in a sort of ecstasy. She could not eat. The dream or vision filled her whole soul, and physical needs were forgotten.

Mr. Garnet said to her :

"Oh, Harriet! Harriet! You've come to torment us before the time; do cease this noise ! My grandchildren may see the day of the emancipation of our people, but you and I will never see it."

"I tell you, sir, you'll see it, and you'll see it soon. My people are free! My people are free."

When, three years later, President Lincoln's proclamation of emancipation was given forth, and there was a great jubilee among the friends of the slaves, Harriet was continually asked, "Why do you not join with the rest in their rejoicing!" "Oh," she answered, "I had *my* jubilee three years ago. I rejoiced all I could den ; I can't rejoice no more."

In some of the Southern States, spies and scouts were needed to lead our armies into the interior. The ignorant and degraded slaves feared the "Yankee Buckra" more than they did their own masters, and after the proclamation of President Lincoln, giving freedom to the slaves, a person in whom these poor creatures could trust, was needed to assure them that these white Northern men were friends, and that they would be safe, trusting themselves in their hands.

In the early days of the war, Governor Andrew of Massachusetts, knowing well the brave and sagacious character of Harriet, sent for her, and asked her if she could go at a moment's notice, to act as

spy and scout for our armies, and, if need be, to
act as hospital nurse, in short, to be ready to give
any required service to the Union cause.

There was much to be thought of ; there were
the old folks in the little home up in Auburn, there
was the little farm of which she had taken the sole
care ; there were many dependents for whom she
had provided by her daily toil.   What was to
become of them all if she deserted them ?   But the
cause of the Union seemed to need her services,
and after a few moments of reflection, she determined to leave all else, and go where it seemed
that duty called her.

During those few years, the wants of the old
people and of Harriet's other dependents were
attended to by the kind people of Auburn.   At
that time, I often saw the old people, and wrote
letters for them to officers at the South, asking
from them tidings of Harriet.   I received many
letters in reply, all testifying to her faithfulness
and bravery, and her untiring zeal for the welfare
of our soldiers, black and white.   She was often
under fire from both armies ; she led our forces
through the jungle and the swamp, guided by an

unseen hand. She gained the confidence of the slaves by her cheery words, and songs, and sacred hymns, and obtained from them much valuable information. She nursed our soldiers in the hospitals, and knew how, when they were dying by numbers of some malignant disease, with cunning skill to extract from roots and herbs, which grew near the source of the disease, the healing draught, which allayed the fever and restored numbers to health.

It is a shame to our government that such a valuable helper as this woman was not allowed pay or pension ; but even was obliged to support herself during those days of incessant toil. Officers and men were paid. Indeed many enlisted from no patriotic motive, but because they were insured a support which they could not procure for themselves at home. But this woman sacrificed everything, and left her nearest and dearest, and risked her life hundreds of times for the cause of the Union, without one cent of recompense. She returned at last to her little home, to find it a scene of desolation. Her little place about to be sold to satisfy a mortgage, and herself without the means to redeem it.

Harriet was one of John Brown's "men." His brave and daring spirit found ready sympathy in her courageous heart; she sheltered him in her home in Canada, and helped him to plan his campaigns. I find in the life and letters of this remarkable man, written by Mr. F. B. Sanborn, occasional mention of Harriet, and her deep interest in Captain Brown's enterprises.

At one time he writes to his son from St. Catherine's, Canada :

"I came on here the day after you left Rochester. I am succeeding to all appearance beyond my expectations. Harriet Tubman *hooked on her whole team at once.* He (Harriet) is the most of a man naturally that I ever met with. There is abundant material here and of the right quality." She suggested the 4th of July to him as the time to begin operations. And Mr. Sanborn adds : "It was about the 4th of July, as Harriet, the African sybil, had suggested, that Brown first showed himself in the counties of Washington and Jefferson, on opposite sides of the lordly Potomac."

I find among her papers, many of which are defaced by being carried about with her for years, portions of these letters addressed to myself, by persons at the South, and speaking of the valuable assistance Harriet was rendering our soldiers in the hospital, and our armies in the field. At this time her manner of life, as related by herself, was this :

"Well, missus, I'd go to de hospital, I would, early eb'ry mornin'. I'd get a big chunk of ice, I would, and put it in a basin, and fill it with water ; den I'd take a sponge and begin. Fust man I'd come to, I'd thrash away de flies, and dey'd rise, dey would, like bees roun' a hive. Den I'd begin to bathe der wounds, an' by de time I'd bathed off three or four, de fire and heat would have melted de ice and made de water warm, an' it would be as red as clar blood. Den I'd go an' git more ice, I would, an' by de time I got to de nex' ones, de flies would be roun' de fust ones black an' thick as eber." In this way she worked, day after day, till late at night ; then she went home to her little cabin, and made about fifty pies, a great quantity of ginger-bread, and two casks of root beer. These she would hire some contraband to sell for her through the camps, and thus she would provide her support for another day ; for this woman never received pay or pension, and never drew for herself but twenty days' rations during the four years of her labors.   At one time she was called away from Hilton Head, by one of our officers, to come to Fernandina, where the men were " dying off like sheep," from dysentery.   Harriet had acquired quite a reputation for her skill in curing this disease, by a medicine which she prepared from roots which grew near the waters which gave the disease. Here she found thousands of sick soldiers and contrabands, and immediately gave up her time and attention to them.   At another time, we find her nursing those who were down by hundreds with small-pox and malignant fevers.   She had never had these diseases, but she seems to have no more fear of death in one form than another.   " De Lord would take keer of her till her time came, an' den she was ready to go."

When our armies and gun-boats first appeared in any part of the South, many of the poor negroes were as much afraid of " de Yankee Buckra " as of their own masters.   It was almost impossible to win their confidence, or to get information from them. But to Harriet they would tell anything ; and so it became quite important that she should accompany expeditions going up the rivers, or into unexplored parts of the country, to control and get information from those whom they took with them as guides.

General Hunter asked her at one time if she would go with several gun-boats up the Combahee River, the object of the expedition being to take up the torpedoes placed by the rebels in the river, to destroy railroads and bridges, and to cut off supplies from the rebel troops. She said she would go if Colonel Montgomery was to be appointed commander of the expedition. Colonel Montgomery was one of John Brown's men, and was well known to Harriet. Accordingly, Colonel Montgomery was appointed to the command, and Harriet, with several men under her, the principal of whom was J. Plowden, whose pass I have, accompanied the expedition. Harriet describes in the most graphic manner the appearance of the plantations as they passed up the river; the frightened negroes leaving their work and taking to the woods, at sight of the gun-boats ; then coming to peer out like startled deer, and scudding away like the wind at the sound of the steam-whistle. " Well," said

one old negro, " Mas'r said de Yankees had horns
and tails, but I nebber beliebed it till now." But
the word was passed along by the mysterious tele-
graphic communication existing among these simple people, that these were " Lincoln's gun-boats
come to set them free." In vain, then, the drivers
used their whips in their efforts to hurry the poor
creatures back to their quarters ; they all turned
and ran for the gun-boats. They came down
every road, across every field, just as they had
left their work and their cabins ; women with
children clinging around their necks, hanging to
their dresses, running behind, all making at full
speed for " Lincoln's gun-boats." Eight hundred
poor wretches at one time crowded the banks,
with their hands extended toward their deliverers,
and they were all taken off upon the gun-boats,
and carried down to Beaufort.

" I nebber see such a sight," said Harriet ; " we
laughed, an' laughed, an' laughed. Here you'd
see a woman wid a pail on her head, rice a smokin'
in it jus' as she'd taken it from de fire, young one
hangin' on behind, one han' roun' her forehead to
hold on, 'tother han' diggin' into de rice-pot, eatin'

wid all its might ; hold of her dress two or three more ; down her back a bag wid a pig in it. One woman brought two pigs, a white one an' a black one ; we took 'em all on board ; named de white pig Beauregard, and de black pig Jeff Davis. Sometimes de women would come wid twins hangin' roun' der necks ; 'pears like I nebber see so many twins in my life ; bags on der shoulders, baskets on der heads, and young ones taggin' behin', all loaded ; pigs squealin', chickens screamin', young ones squallin'." And so they came pouring down to the gun-boats. When they stood on the shore, and the small boats put out to take them off, they all wanted to get in at once. After the boats were crowded, they would hold on to them so that they could not leave the shore. The oarsmen would beat them on their hands, but they would not let go ; they were afraid the gun-boats would go off and leave them, and all wanted to make sure of one of these arks of refuge. At length Colonel Montgomery shouted from the upper deck, above the clamor of appealing tones, " Moses, you'll have to give em a song." Then Harriet lifted up her voice, and sang:

" Of all the whole creation in the East or in the West,
    The glorious Yankee nation is the greatest and the best.
    Come along!   Come along ! don't be alarmed,
    Uncle Sam is rich enough to give you all a farm."

At the end of every verse, the negroes in their
enthusiasm would throw up their hands and shout
" Glory," and the row-boats would take that op-
portunity to push off ; and so at last they were all
brought on board.   The masters fled ; houses and
barns and railroad bridges were burned, tracks
torn up, torpedoes destroyed, and the object of the
expedition was fully accomplished.

This fearless woman was often sent into the
rebel lines as a spy, and brought back valuable
information as to the position of armies and bat-
teries ; she has been in battle when the shot was
falling like hail, and the bodies of dead and
wounded men were dropping around her like
leaves in autumn ; but the thought of fear never
seems to have had place for a moment in her
mind.   She had her duty to perform, and she
expected to be taken care of till it was done.

Would that, instead of taking them in this poor
way at second-hand, my readers could hear this

woman's graphic accounts of scenes she herself witnessed, could listen to her imitations of negro preachers in their own very peculiar dialect, her singing of camp-meeting hymns, her account of "experience meetings," her imitations of the dances, and the funeral ceremonies of these simple people. "Why, der language down dar in de far South is jus' as different from ours in Maryland as you can tink," said she. "Dey laughed when dey heard me talk, an' I could not understand dem, no how." She described a midnight funeral which she attended ; for the slaves, never having been allowed to bury their dead in the day-time, continued the custom of night funerals from habit.

The corpse was laid upon the ground, and the people all sat round, the group being lighted up by pine torches.

The old negro preacher began by giving out a hymn, which was sung by all. "An' oh ! I wish you could hear 'em sing, Missus," said Harriet. "Der voices is so sweet, and dey can sing eberyting we sing, an' den dey can sing a great many hymns dat we can't nebber catch at all."

The old preacher began his sermon by pointing

to the dead man, who lay in a rude box on the ground before him.

" *Shum ?* Ded-a-de-dah! *Shum, David ?* Ded-a-de-dah! Now I want you all to *flec'* for moment. Who ob all dis congregation is gwine next to lie ded-e-de-dah? You can't go nowhere's, my frien's and bredren, but Deff 'll fin' you. You can't dig no hole so deep an' bury yourself dar, but God A'mighty's far-seein' eye 'll fin' you, an' Deff 'll come arter you. You can't go into that big fort (pointing to Hilton Head), an' shut yourself up dar; dat fort dat Sesh Buckra said the debil couldn't take, but Deff 'll fin' you dar. All your frien's may forget you, but Deff 'll nebber forget you. Now, my bredren, prepare to lie ded-a-de-dah!"

This was the burden of a very long sermon, after which the whole congregation went round in a sort of solemn dance, called the " spiritual shuffle," shaking hands with each other, and calling each other by name as they sang :

" My sis'r Mary's boun' to go ;
My sis'r Nanny's boun' to go ;
My brudder Tony's boun' to go ;
My brudder July's boun' to go."

This to the same tune, till every hand had been shaken by every one of the company. When they came to Harriet, who was a stranger, they sang:

Eberybody's boun' to go !

The body was then placed in a Government wagon, and by the light of the pine torches, the strange, dark procession moved along, singing a rude funeral hymn, till they reached the place of burial.

Harriet's account of her interview with an old negro she met at Hilton Head, is amusing and interesting. He said, " I'd been yere seventy-three years, workin' for my master widout even a dime wages. I'd worked rain-wet sun-dry. I'd worked wid my mouf full of dust, but could not stop to get a drink of water. I'd been whipped, an' starved, an' I was always prayin', 'Oh ! Lord, come an' delibber us !' All dat time de birds had been flyin', an' de rabens had been cryin', and de fish had been swimmin' in de waters. One day I look up, an' I see a big cloud; it didn't come up like as de clouds come out far yonder, but it 'peared to be right ober head. Der was thunders out of dat, an' der was lightnin's. Den I looked down on de water, an' I see, 'peared to me a big house in de water, an' out of de big house came great big eggs, and de good eggs went on trou' de air, an' fell into de fort ; an' de bad eggs burst before dey got dar. Den de Sesh Buckra begin to run, an' de neber stop running till de git to de swamp, an' de stick dar an' de die dar. Den I heard 'twas de Yankee ship * firin' out de big eggs, an dey had come to set us free. Den I praise de Lord. He come an' put he little finger in de work, an de Sesh Buckra all go ; and de birds stop flyin', and de rabens stop cryin', an' when I go to catch a fish to eat wid my rice, dey's no fish dar. De Lord A'mighty 'd come and frightened 'em all out of de waters. Oh ! Praise de Lord ! I 'd prayed seventy-three years, an' now he 's come an' we's all free."

The following account of the subject of this memoir is cut from the *Boston Commonwealth* of 1863, kindly sent the writer by Mr. Sanborn:

" It was said long ago that the true romance of America was not in the fortunes of the Indian, where Cooper sought it, nor in New England character, where Judd found it, nor in the social

---

* The *Wabash.*

contrasts of Virginia planters, as Thackeray imagined, but in the story of the fugitive slaves. The observation is as true now as it was before War, with swift, gigantic hand, sketched the vast shadows, and dashed in the high lights in which romance loves to lurk and flash forth. But the stage is enlarged on which these dramas are played, the whole world now sit as spectators, and the desperation or the magnanimity of a poor black woman has power to shake the nation that so long was deaf to her cries. We write of one of these heroines, of whom our slave annals are full —a woman whose career is as extraordinary as the most famous of her sex can show.

"Araminta Ross, now known by her married name of Tubman, with her sounding Christian name changed to Harriet, is the grand-daughter of a slave imported from Africa, and has not a drop of white blood in her veins. Her parents were Benjamin Ross and Harriet Greene, both slaves, but married and faithful to each other. They still live in old age and poverty,* but free, on a little property at Auburn, N. Y., which their daughter

* Both dead for some years.

purchased for them from Mr. Seward, the Secretary
of State. She was born, as near as she can remember, in 1820 or in 1821, in Dorchester County, on
the Eastern shore of Maryland, and not far from
the town of Cambridge. She had ten brothers and
sisters, of whom three are now living, all at the
North, and all rescued from slavery by Harriet, before the War. She went back just as the South
was preparing to secede, to bring away a fourth,
but before she could reach her, she was dead.
Three years before, she had brought away her old
father and mother, at great risk to herself.

"When Harriet was six years old, she was taken
from her mother and carried ten miles to live with
James Cook, whose wife was a weaver, to learn
the trade of weaving. While still a mere child,
Cook set her to watching his musk-rat traps, which
compelled her to wade through the water. It happened that she was once sent when she was ill with
the measles, and, taking cold from wading in the
water in this condition, she grew very sick, and her
mother persuaded her master to take her away
from Cook's until she could get well.

"Another attempt was made to teach her weaving, but she would not learn, for she hated her mistress, and did not want to live at home, as she would have done as a weaver, for it was the custom then to weave the cloth for the family, or a part of it, in the house.

"Soon after she entered her teens she was hired out as a field hand, and it was while thus employed that she received a wound, which nearly proved fatal, from the effects of which she still suffers. In the fall of the year, the slaves there work in the evening, cleaning up wheat, husking corn, etc. On this occasion, one of the slaves of a farmer named Barrett, left his work, and went to the village store in the evening. The overseer followed him, and so did Harriet. When the slave was found, the overseer swore he should be whipped, and called on Harriet, among others, to help tie him. She refused, and as the man ran away, she placed herself in the door to stop pursuit. The overseer caught up a two-pound weight from the counter and threw it at the fugitive, but it fell short and struck Harriet a stunning blow on the head. It was long before she recovered from this, and it has left her subject to a sort of stupor or lethargy at times ; coming upon her in the midst of conversation, or whatever she may be doing, and throwing her into a deep slumber, from which she will presently rouse herself, and go on with her conversation or work.

" After this she lived for five or six years with John Stewart, where at first she worked in the house, but afterward 'hired her time,' and Dr. Thompson, son of her master's guardian, 'stood for her,' that is, was her surety for the payment of what she owed.   She employed the time thus hired in the rudest labors,—drove oxen, carted, plowed, and did all the work of a man,—sometimes earning money enough in a year, beyond what she paid her master, 'to buy a pair of steers,' worth forty dollars.   The amount exacted of a woman for her time was fifty or sixty dollars—of a man, one hundred to one hundred and fifty dollars.   Frequently Harriet worked for her father, who was a timber inspector, and superintended the cutting and hauling of great quantities of timber for the Baltimore ship-yards.   Stewart, his temporary master, was a builder, and for the work of Ross used to receive as much as five dollars a day sometimes, he being a superior workman. While engaged with her father, she would cut wood, haul logs, etc. Her usual 'stint' was half a cord of wood in a day.

"Harriet was married somewhere about 1844, to a free colored man named John Tubman, but she had no children. For the last two years of slavery she lived with Dr. Thompson, before mentioned, her own master not being yet of age, and Dr. T.'s father being his guardian, as well as the owner of her own father. In 1849 the young man died, and the slaves were to be sold, though previously set free by an old will. Harriet resolved not to be sold, and so, with no knowledge of the North—having only heard of Pennsylvania and New Jersey—she walked away one night alone. She found a friend in a white lady, who knew her story and helped her on her way. After many adventures, she reached Philadelphia, where she found work and earned a small stock of money. With this money in her purse, she traveled back to Maryland for her husband, but she found him married to another woman, and no longer caring to live with her. This, however, was not until two years after her escape, for she does not seem to have reached

her old home in the first two expeditions. In
December, 1850, she had visited Baltimore and
brought away her sister and two children, who had
come up from Cambridge in a boat, under charge
of her sister's husband, a free black. A few months
after she had brought away her brother and two
other men, but it was not till the fall of 1851, that
she found her husband and learned of his infidelity.
She did not give way to rage or grief, but collected
a party of fugitives and brought them safely to
Philadelphia. In December of the same year, she
returned, and led out a party of eleven, among
them her brother and his wife. With these she
journeyed to Canada, and there spent the winter,
for this was after the enforcement of Mason's Fugitive Slave Bill in Philadelphia and Boston, and
there was no safety except 'under the paw of the
British Lion,' as she quaintly said. But the first
winter was terribly severe for these poor runaways.
They earned their bread by chopping wood in the
snows of a Canadian forest ; they were frost-bitten,
hungry, and naked. Harriet was their good angel.
She kept house for her brother, and the poor
creatures boarded with her. She worked for them,

begged for them, prayed for them, with the strange familiarity of communion with God which seems natural to these people, and cairied them by the help of God through the hard winter.

"In the spring she returned to the States, and as usual earned money by working in hotels and families as a cook. From Cape May, in the fall of 1852, she went back once more to Maryland, and brought away nine more fugitives.

"Up to this time she had expended chiefly her own money in these expeditions—money which she had earned by hard work in the drudgery of the kitchen. Never did any one more exactly fulfill the sense of George Herbert—

" ' A servant with this clause
Makes drudgery divine.'

"But it was not possible for such virtues long to remain hidden from the keen eyes of the Abolitionists. She became known to Thomas Garrett, the large-hearted Quaker of Wilmington, who has aided the escape of three thousand fugitives ; she found warm friends in Philadelphia and New York, and wherever she went. These gave her money, which

she never spent for her own use, but laid up for
the help of her people, and especially for her journeys back to the 'land of Egypt,' as she called her
old home. By reason of her frequent visits there,
always carrying away some of the oppressed, she
got among her people the name of 'Moses,' which
it seems she still retains.

"Between 1852 and 1857, she made but two of
these journeys, in consequence partly of the increased vigilance of the slave-holders, who had suffered so much by the loss of their property. A
great reward was offered for her capture and she
several times was on the point of being taken, but
always escaped by her quick wit, or by 'warnings'
from Heaven—for it is time to notice one singular
trait in her character. She is the most shrewd and
practical person in the world, yet she is a firm be-
liever in omens, dreams, and warnings. She declares that before her escape from slavery, she
used to dream of flying over fields and towns, and
rivers and mountains, looking down upon them
'like a bird,' and reaching at last a great fence, or
sometimes a river, over which she would try to fly,
'but it 'peared like I wouldn't hab de strength, and

jes as I was sinkin' down, dere would be ladies all drest in white ober dere, and dey would put out dere arms and pull me 'cross.' There is nothing strange in this, perhaps, but she declares that when she came North she remembered these very places as those she had seen in her dreams, and many of the ladies who befriended her were those she had been helped by in her vision.

" Then she says she always knows when there is danger near her—she does not know how, exactly, but ' 'pears like my heart go flutter, flutter, and den dey may say " Peace, Peace," as much as dey likes, *I know its gwine to be war !* ' She is very firm on this point, and ascribes to this her great impunity, in spite of the lethargy before mentioned, which would seem likely to throw her into the hands of her enemies. She says she inherited this power, that her father could always predict the weather, and that he foretold the Mexican war.

"In 1857 she made her most venturesome jour-ney, for she brought with her to the North her old parents, who were no longer able to walk such dis-tances as she must go by night. Consequently she must hire a wagon for them, and it required all her

ingenuity to get them through Maryland and Delaware safe.   She accomplished it, however, and by
the aid of her friends she brought them safe to
Canada, where they spent the winter.   Her account
of their sufferings there—of her mother's complain-
ing and her own philosophy about it—is a lesson
of trust in Providence better than many sermons.
But she decided to bring them to a more comforta-
ble place, and so she negotiated with Mr. Seward
—then in the Senate—for a little patch of ground.
To the credit of the Secretary of State it should be
said, that he sold her the property on very favora-
ble terms, and gave her some time for payment.   To
this house she removed her parents, and set herself
to work to pay for the purchase.   It was on this
errand that she first visited Boston—we believe in
the winter of 1858–59.   She brought a few letters
from her friends in New York, but she could herself neither read nor write, and she was obliged
to trust to her wits that they were delivered to the
right persons.   One of them, as it happened, was
to the present writer, who received it by another
hand, and called to see her at her boarding-house.
It was curious to see the caution with which she re-

ceived her visitor until she felt assured that there
was no mistake. One of her means of security
was to carry with her the daguerreotypes of her
friends, and show them to each new person. If
they recognized the likeness, then it was all right.

"Pains were taken to secure her the attention to
which her great services of humanity entitled her,
and she left New England with a handsome sum
of money toward the payment of her debt to Mr.
Seward. Before she left, however, she had several
interviews with Captain Brown, then in Boston.
He is supposed to have communicated his plans to
her, and to have been aided by her in obtaining re-
cruits and money among her people. At any rate,
he always spoke of her with the greatest respect,
and declared that 'General Tubman,' as he styled
her, was a better officer than most whom he had
seen, and could command an army as successfully
as she had led her small parties of fugitives.

"Her own veneration for Captain Brown has
always been profound, and since his murder, has
taken the form of a religion. She had often risked
her own life for her people, and she thought nothing
of that ; but that a white man, and a man so noble

and strong, should so take upon himself the burden of a despised race, she could not understand,
and she took refuge from her perplexity in the
mysteries of her fervid religion.

"Again, she laid great stress on a dream which
she had just before she met Captain Brown in Canada. She thought she was in ' a wilderness sort of
place, all full of rocks, and bushes,' when she saw a
serpent raise its head among the rocks, and as it
did so, it became the head of an old man with a
long white beard, gazing at her, 'wishful like, jes
as ef he war gwine to speak to me,' and then two
other heads rose up beside him, younger than he,—
and as she stood looking at them, and wondering
what they could want with her, a great crowd of
men rushed in and struck down the younger heads,
and then the head of the old man, still looking at
her so ' wishful.' This dream she had again and
again, and could not interpret it ; but when she
met Captain Brown, shortly after, behold, he was
the very image of the head she had seen. But still
she could not make out what her dream signified,
till the news came to her of the tragedy of Harper's Ferry, and then she knew the two other heads

were his two sons. She was in New York at that time, and on the day of the affair at Harper's Ferry she felt her usual warning that something was wrong—she could not tell what. Finally she told her hostess that it must be Captain Brown who was in trouble, and that they should soon hear bad news from him. The next day's newspaper brought tidings of what had happened.

" Her last visit to Maryland was made after this, in December, 1860 ; and in spite of the agitated condition of the country, and the greater watchfulness of the slave-holders, she brought away seven fugitives, one of them an infant, which must be drugged with opium to keep it from crying on the way, and so revealing the hiding-place of the party."

In the spring of 1860, Harriet Tubman was requested by Mr. Gerrit Smith to go to Boston to attend a large Anti-Slavery meeting. On her way, she stopped at Troy to visit a cousin, and while there the colored people were one day startled with the intelligence that a fugitive slave, by the name of Charles Nalle, had been followed by his master (who was his younger brother, and not one grain whiter than he), and that he was already in the hands of the officers, and was to be taken back to the South. The instant Harriet heard the news, she started for the office of the United States Commissioner, scattering the tidings as she went. An excited crowd was gathered about the office, through which Harriet forced her way, and rushed up stairs to the door of the room where the fugitive was detained. A wagon was already waiting before the door to carry off the man, but the crowd was even then so great, and in such a state of excitement, that the officers did not dare to bring the man down. On the opposite side of the street stood the colored people, watching the window where they could see Harriet's sun-bonnet, and feeling assured that so long as she stood there, the fugitive was still in the office. Time passed on, and he did not appear. "They've taken him out another way, depend upon that," said some of the colored people. " No," replied others, "there stands ' Moses ' yet, and as long as she is there, he is safe." Harriet, now seeing the necessity for a tremendous effort for his rescue, sent out some little boys to cry *fire*. The bells rang, the crowd increased, till the whole street was a dense mass of people. Again and again the officers came out to try and clear the stairs, and make a way to take their captive down ; others were driven down, but Harriet stood her ground, her head bent and her arms folded. " Come, old woman, you must get out of this," said one of the officers ; " I must have the way cleared ; if you can't get down alone, some one will help you." Harriet, still putting on a greater appearance of decrepitude, twitched away from him, and kept her place. Offers were made to buy Charles from his master, who at first agreed to take twelve hundred dollars for him ; but when this was subscribed, he immediately raised the price to fifteen hundred. The crowd grew more excited. A gentleman raised a window and called out, " Two hundred dollars for his rescue, but not one cent to his master ! " This was responded to by a roar of satisfaction from the crowd below. At length the officers appeared, and announced to the crowd, that if they would open a lane to the wagon, they would promise to bring the man down the front way.

The lane was opened, and the man was brought

out—a tall, handsome, intelligent *white* man, with his wrists manacled together, walking between the U. S. Marshal and another officer, and behind him his brother and his master, so like him that one could hardly be told from the other. The moment they appeared, Harriet roused from her stooping posture, threw up a window, and cried to her friends : " Here he comes—take him !" and then darted down the stairs like a wild-cat. She seized one officer and pulled him down, then another, and tore him away from the man ; and keeping her arms about the slave, she cried to her friends : " Drag us out ! Drag him to the river ! Drown him ! but don't let them have him !" They were knocked down together, and while down, she tore off her sun-bonnet and tied it on the head of the fugitive. When he rose, only his head could be seen, and amid the surging mass of people the slave was no longer recognized, while the master appeared like the slave. Again and again they were knocked down, the poor slave utterly helpless, with his manacled wrists, streaming with blood. Harriet's outer clothes were torn from her, and even her stout shoes were pulled from her feet,

yet she never relinquished her hold of the man,
till she had dragged him to the river, where he
was tumbled into a boat, Harriet following in a
ferry-boat to the other side. But the telegraph was
ahead of them, and as soon as they landed he was
seized and hurried from her sight. After a time,
some school children came hurrying along, and to
her anxious inquiries they answered, " He is up in
that house, in the third story." Harriet rushed up
to the place. Some men were attempting to make
their way up the stairs. The officers were firing
down, and two men were lying on the stairs, who
had been shot. Over their bodies our heroine
rushed, and with the help of others burst open the
door of the room, and dragged out the fugitive,
whom Harriet carried down stairs in her arms. A
gentleman who was riding by with a fine horse,
stopped to ask what the disturbance meant ; and
on hearing the story, his sympathies seemed to be
thoroughly aroused ; he sprang from his wagon,
calling out, " That is a blood-horse, drive him till
he drops." The poor man was hurried in ; some of
his friends jumped in after him, and drove at the
most rapid rate to Schenectady.

This is the story Harriet told to the writer. By some persons it seemed too wonderful for belief, and an attempt was made to corroborate it. Rev. Henry Fowler, who was at the time at Saratoga, kindly volunteered to go to Troy and ascertain the facts. His report was, that he had had a long interview with Mr. Townsend, who acted during the trial as counsel for the slave, that he had given him a "rich narration," which he would write out the next week for this little book. But before he was to begin his generous labor, and while engaged in some kind efforts for the prisoners at Auburn, he was stricken down by the heat of the sun, and was for a long time debarred from labor.

This good man died not long after and the promised narration was never written, but a statement by Mr. Townsend was sent me, which I copy here:

Statements made by Martin I. Townsend, Esq., of Troy, who was counsel for the fugitive, Charles Nalle.

Nalle is an octoroon ; his wife has the same infusion of Caucasian blood. She was the daughter of her master, and had, with her sister, been bred by him in his family, as his own child. When the father died, both of these daughters were married and had large families of children. Under the highly Christian national laws of " Old Virginny," these children were the slaves of their grandfather. The old man died, leaving a will, whereby he manumitted his daughters and their children, and provided for the purchase of the freedom of their husbands. The manumission of the children and grandchildren took effect ; but the estate was insufficient to purchase the husbands of his daughters, and the fathers of his grandchildren. The manumitted, by another Christian, "conservative," and "national" provision of law, were forced to leave the State, while the slave husbands remained in slavery. Nalle, and his brother-in-law, were allowed for a while to visit their families outside Virginia about once a year, but were at length ordered to provide themselves with new wives, as they would be allowed to visit their former ones no more. It was after this that Nalle and his brother-in-law started for the land of freedom, guided by the steady light of the north star. Thank God, neither family now need fear any earthly master or the bay of the blood-hound dogging their fugitive steps.

Nalle returned to Troy with his family about July, 1860, and resided with them there for more than seven years. They are all now residents of the city of Washington, D. C. Nalle and his family are persons of refined manners, and of the highest respectability. Several of his children are red-haired, and a stranger would discover no trace of African blood in their complexions or features. It was the head of this family whom H. F. Averill proposed to doom to returnless exile and life-long slavery.

When Nalle was brought from Commissioner Beach's office into the street, Harriet Tubman, who had been standing with the excited crowd, rushed amongst the foremost to Nalle, and running one of her arms around his manacled arm, held on to him without ever loosening her hold through the more than half-hour's struggle to Judge Gould's office, and from Judge Gould's office to the dock, where Nalle's liberation was accomplished. In the *mêlée* she was repeatedly beaten over the head with policemen's clubs, but she never for a moment released her hold, but cheered Nalle and his friends with her voice, and struggled with the officers until they were literally worn out with their exertions, and Nalle was separated from them.

True, she had strong and earnest helpers in her struggle, some of whom had white faces as well as human hearts, and are now in Heaven. But she exposed herself to the fury of the sympathizers with slavery, without fear, and suffered their blows without flinching. Harriet crossed the river with the crowd, in the ferry-boat, and when the men who led the assault upon the door of Judge Stewart's office were stricken down, Harriet and a number of other colored women rushed over their bodies, brought Nalle out, and putting him in the first wagon passing, started him for the West.

A lively team, driven by a colored man, was immediately sent on to relieve the other, and Nalle was seen about Troy no more until he returned a free man by purchase from his master. Harriet also disappeared, and the crowd dispersed. How she came to be in Troy that day, is entirely unknown to our citizens; and where she hid herself after the rescue, is equally a mystery. But her struggle was in the sight of a thousand, perhaps of five thousand spectators.

On asking Harriet particularly, as to the age of her mother, she answered, "Well, I'll tell you, Missus. Twenty-three years ago, in Maryland, I paid a lawyer five dollars to look up the will of my mother's first master. He looked back sixty years, and said it was time to give up. I told him to go back furder. He went back sixty-five years, and there he found the will—giving the girl Ritty to his grand-daughter (Mary Patterson), to serve her and her offspring till she was forty-five years of age." This grand-daughter died soon after, unmarried; and as there was no provision for Ritty, in case of her death, she was actually emancipated at that time. But no one informed her of the fact, and she and her dear children remained in bondage till emancipated by the courage and determination of this heroic daughter and sister. The old woman must then, it seems, be ninety-eight years of age,* and the old man has probably numbered as many years.

---

* This was written in the year '68, and the old people both lived several years after that time.

And yet these old people, living out beyond the toll-gate, on the South Street road, Auburn, come in every Sunday—more than a mile—to the Central Church. To be sure, deep slumbers settle down upon them as soon as they are seated, which continue undisturbed till the congregation is dismissed ; but they have done their best, and who can doubt that they receive a blessing. Immediately after this they go to class-meeting at the Methodist Church. Then they wait for a third service, and after that start out home again.

Harriet supposes that the whole family were actually free, and were kept wrongfully in a state of slavery all those long years ; but she simply states the fact, without any mourning or lamenting over the wrong and the misery of it all, accepting it as the will of God, and, therefore, not to be rebelled against.

This woman, of whom you have been reading, is now old and feeble, suffering from the effects of her life of unusual labor and hardship, as well as from repeated injuries ; but she is still at work for her people. For many years, even long before the war, her little home has been the refuge of the hunted and the homeless, for whom she had provided ; and I have seen as many as eight or ten dependents upon her care at one time living there.

It has always been a hospital, but she feels the need of a large one, and only prays to see this, " her last work," completed ere she goes hence.

Without claiming any of my dear old Harriet's prophetic vision, I seem to see a future day when the wrongs of earth will be righted, and justice, long delayed, will assert itself.   I seem to see that our poor Harriet has passed within " one of dem gates," and has received the welcome, "Come, thou blessed of my Father; for I was hungry and you gave me meat, I was thirsty and you gave me drink, I was a stranger and you took me in, naked and you clothed me, sick and in prison and you visited me."

And when she asks, " Lord, when did I do all this ? "   He answers :

" Inasmuch as you did it unto one of the least of these, *my brethren*, you did it unto me."

And as she stands in her modest way just within the celestial gate, I seem to see a kind hand laid upon her dark head, and to hear a gentle voice saying in her ear, "Friend, come up higher!"

APPENDIX.

THE following letters to the writer from those well-known and distinguished philanthropists, Hon. Gerrit Smith and Wendell Phillips, and one from Frederick Douglass, addressed to Harriet, will serve as the best introduction that can be given of the subject of this memoir to its readers:

Letter from Hon. Gerrit Smith.

PETERBORO, *June* 13, 1868.

MY DEAR MADAME: I am happy to learn that you are to speak to the public of Mrs. Harriet Tubman. Of the remarkable events of her life I have no *personal* knowledge, but of the truth of them as she describes them I have no doubt.

I have often listened to her, in her visits to my family, and I am confident that she is not only truthful, but that she has a rare discernment, and a deep and sublime philanthropy.

With great respect your friend,

GERRIT SMITH.

Letter from Wendell Phillips.

June 16, 1868.

DEAR MADAME: The last time I ever saw John Brown was under my own roof, as he brought Harriet

Tubman to me, saying: " Mr. Phillips, I bring you one of the best and bravest persons on this continent—*General* Tubman, as we call her."

He then went on to recount her labors and sacrifices in behalf of her race. After that, Harriet spent some time in Boston, earning the confidence and admiration of all those who were working for freedom. With their aid she went to the South more than once, returning always with a squad of self-emancipated men, women, and children, for whom her marvelous skill had opened the way of escape. After the war broke out, she was sent with indorsements from Governor Andrew and his friends to South Carolina, where in the service of the Nation she rendered most important and efficient aid to our army.

In my opinion there are few captains, perhaps few colonels, who have done more for the loyal cause since the war began, and few men who did before that time more for the colored race, than our fearless and most sagacious friend, Harriet.

Faithfully yours,

WENDELL PHILLIPS.

Letter from Frederick Douglass.

ROCHESTER, *August* 29, 1868.

DEAR HARRIET: I am glad to know that the story of your eventful life has been written by a kind lady, and that the same is soon to be published. You ask for what you do not need when you call upon me for a word of commendation. I need such words from you far more than you can need them from me, especially where your superior labors and devotion to the cause of the lately enslaved of our land are known as I know them. The difference between us is very marked. Most that I have done and suffered in the service of our cause has been in public, and I have received much encouragement at every step of the way. You, on the other hand, have labored in a private way. I have wrought in the day— you in the night. I have had the applause of the crowd and the satisfaction that comes of being approved by the multitude, while the most that you have done has been witnessed by a few trembling, scarred, and foot-sore bondmen and women, whom you have led out of the house of bondage, and whose heartfelt " *God bless you* " has been your only reward. The midnight sky and the silent stars have been the witnesses of your devotion to freedom and of your heroism. Excepting John Brown— of sacred memory—I know of no one who has willingly encountered more perils and hardships to serve our enslaved people than you have. Much that you have done would seem improbable to those who do not know you as I know you. It is to me a great pleasure and a great privilege to bear testimony to your character and your works, and to say to those to whom you may come, that I regard you in every way truthful and trustworthy.

Your friend,

FREDERICK DOUGLASS.

Extracts from a Letter written by Mr. Sanborn, Secretary of the Massachusetts Board of State Charities.

MY DEAR MADAME: Mr. Phillips has sent me your

note, asking for reminiscences of Harriet Tubman, and testimonials to her extraordinary story, which all her New England friends will, I am sure, be glad to furnish.

I never had reason to doubt the truth of what Harriet said in regard to her own career, for I found her singularly truthful. Her imagination is warm and rich, and there is a whole region of the marvelous in her nature, which has manifested itself at times remarkably. Her dreams and visions, misgivings and forewarnings, ought not to be omitted in any life of her, particularly those relating to John Brown.

She was in his confidence in 1858–9, and he had a great regard for her, which he often expressed to me. She aided him in his plans, and expected to do so still further, when his career was closed by that wonderful campaign in Virginia. The first time she came to my house, in Concord, after that tragedy, she was shown into a room in the evening, where Brackett's bust of John Brown was standing. The sight of it, which was new to her, threw her into a sort of ecstacy of sorrow and admiration, and she went on in her rhapsodical way to pronounce his apotheosis.

She has often been in Concord, where she resided at the houses of Emerson, Alcott, the Whitneys, the Brooks family, Mrs. Horace Mann, and other well-known persons. They all admired and respected her, and nobody doubted the reality of her adventures. She was too *real* a person to be suspected. In 1862, I think it was, she went from Boston to Port Royal, under the advice and encouragement of Mr. Garrison, Governor Andrew, Dr.

Howe, and other leading people. Her career in South
Carolina is well known to some of our officers, and I
think to Colonel Higginson, now of Newport, R. I.,
and Colonel James Montgomery, of Kansas, to both of whom
she was useful as a spy and guide, if I mistake not. I
regard her as, on the whole, the most extraordinary person of her race I have ever met. She is a negro of pure,
or almost pure blood, can neither read nor write, and
has the characteristics of her race and condition. But
she has done what can scarcely be credited on the best
authority, and she has accomplished her purposes with a
coolness, foresight, patience and wisdom, which in a
white man would have raised him to the highest pitch
of reputation.

I am, dear Madame, very truly your servant,

F. B. SANBORN.

Letter from Hon. Wm. H. Seward.

WASHINGTON, *July* 25, 1868.

MAJ.-GEN. HUNTER—

MY DEAR SIR : Harriet Tubman, a colored woman,
has been nursing our soldiers during nearly all the war.
She believes she has a claim for faithful services to the
command in South Carolina with which you are connected, and she thinks that you would be disposed to
see her claim justly settled.

I have known her long, and a nobler, higher spirit, or
a truer, seldom dwells in the human form. I commend
her, therefore, to your kind and best attentions.

Faithfully your friend,

WILLIAM H. SEWARD.

Letter from Col. James Montgomery.

ST. HELENA ISLAND, S. C., *July* 6, 1863.
HEADQUARTERS COLORED BRIGADE.

BRIG.-GEN. GILMORE, Commanding Department of the
South—

GENERAL : I wish to commend to your attention, Mrs.
Harriet Tubman, a most remarkable woman, and in-
valuable as a scout. I have been acquainted with her
character and actions for several years.

I am, General, your most ob't servant,
JAMES MONTGOMERY, Col. Com. Brigade.

Letter from Mrs. Gen. A. Baird.

PETERBORO, *Nov.* 24, 1864.

The bearer of this, Harriet Tubman, a most excellent
woman, who has rendered faithful and good services to
our Union army, not only in the hospital, but in various
capacities, having been employed under Government at
Hilton Head, and in Florida; and I commend her to the
protection of all officers in whose department she may
happen to be.

She has been known and esteemed for years by the
family of my uncle, Hon. Gerrit Smith, as a person of
great rectitude and capabilities.

MRS. GEN. A. BAIRD.

Letter from Hon. Gerrit Smith.

PETERBORO, N. Y., *Nov.* 4, 1867.

I have known Mrs. Harriet Tubman for many years.

Seldom, if ever, have I met with a person more philan-
thropic, more self-denying, and of more bravery. Nor
must I omit to say that she combines with her sublime
spirit, remarkable discernment and judgment.

During the late war, Mrs. Tubman was eminently
faithful and useful to the cause of our country. She is
poor and has poor parents. Such a servant of the
country should be well paid by the country. I hope
that the Government will look into her case.

GERRIT SMITH.

Testimonial from Gerrit Smith.

PETERBORO, *Nov.* 22, 1864.

The bearer, Harriet Tubman, needs not any recom-
mendation. Nearly all the nation over, she has been
heard of for her wisdom, integrity, patriotism, and
bravery. The cause of freedom owes her much. The
country owes her much.

I have known Harriet for many years, and I hold her
in my high esteem. GERRIT SMITH.

------

*Certificate from Henry K. Durrant, Acting Asst.
Surgeon, U. S. A.*

I certify that I have been acquainted with Harriet
Tubman for nearly two years; and my position as Medical Officer in charge of " contrabands " in this town and
in hospital, has given me frequent and ample opportuni-
ties to observe her general deportment; particularly her
kindness and attention to the sick and suffering of her

own race. I take much pleasure in testifying to the esteem in which she is generally held.

HENRY K. DURRANT,

Acting Assistant Surgeon, U. S. A.

In charge "Contraband" Hospital.

Dated at Beaufort, S. C., the 3d day of May, 1864.

I concur fully in the above.

R. SAXTON, Brig.-Gen. Vol.

The following are a few of the passes used by Harriet throughout the war. Many others are so defaced that it is impossible to decipher them.

HEADQUARTERS DEPARTMENT OF THE SOUTH,

HILTON HEAD, PORT ROYAL, S. C., *Feb.* 19, 1863.

Pass the bearer, Harriet Tubman, to Beaufort and back to this place, and wherever she wishes to go ; and give her free passage at all times, on all Government transports. Harriet was sent to me from Boston by Governor Andrew, of Massachusetts, and is a valuable woman. She has permission, as a servant of the Government, to purchase such provisions from the Commissary as she may need. D. HUNTER, Maj.-Gen. Com.

General Gilmore, who succeeded General Hunter in command of the Department of the South, appends his signature to the same pass.

HEADQUARTERS OF THE DEPARTMENT OF THE SOUTH,
July 1, 1863.
Continued in force.
Q. A. GILMORE, Brig.-Gen. Com.

———

BEAUFORT, *Aug.* 28, 1862.
Will Capt. Warfield please let "Moses" have a little
Bourbon whiskey for medicinal purposes.
HENRY K. DURANT, Act. Ass. Surgeon.

———

WAR DEPARTMENT, WASHINGTON, D. C.,
March 20, 1865.
Pass Mrs. Harriet Tubman (colored) to Hilton Head
and Charleston, S. C., with free transportation on a Gov-
ernment transport,
By order of the Sec. of War.
LOUIS H., Asst. Adj.-Gen., U. S. A.
To Bvt. Brig.-Gen. Van Vliet, U. S. Q. M., N. Y.
Not transferable.

———

WAR DEPARTMENT, WASHINGTON, D. C.,
July 22, 1865.
Permit Harriet Tubman to proceed to Fortress Mon-
roe, Va., on a Government transport. Transportation
will be furnished free of cost.
By order of the Secretary of War.
L. H., Asst. Adj.-Gen.
Not transferable.

Appointment as Nurse.

SIR: I have the honor to inform you that the Medical Director Department of Virginia has been instructed to appoint Harriet Tubman nurse or matron at the Colored Hospital, Fort Monroe, Va.

Very respectfully, your obdt. servant,

V. K. BARNES, Surgeon-General.

Hon. WM. H. SEWARD,

Secretary of State, Washington, D. C.

Of the many letters, testimonials, and passes, placed in the hands of the writer by Harriet, the following are selected for insertion in this book, and are quite sufficient to verify her statements.

A Letter from Gen. Saxton to a lady of Auburn.

ATLANTA, GA., *March* 21, 1868.

MY DEAR MADAME: I have just received your letter informing me that Hon. Wm. H. Seward, Secretary of State, would present a petition to Congress for a pension to Harriet Tubman, for services rendered in the Union Army during the late war. I can bear witness to the value of her services in South Carolina and Florida. She was employed in the hospitals and as a spy. She made many a raid inside the enemy's lines, displaying remarkable courage, zeal, and fidelity. She was employed by General Hunter, and I think by Generals Stevens and Sherman, and is as deserving of a pension from the Government for her services as any other of its faithful servants.

I am very truly yours,

RUFUS SAXTON, Bvt. Brig.-Gen., U. S. A.

Rev. Samuel I. May, in his recollections of the anti-slavery conflict, after mentioning the case of an old slave mother, whom he vainly endeavored to assist her son in buying from her master, says :

"I did not until four years after know that remarkable woman Harriet, or I might have engaged her services, in the assurance that she would have bought off the old woman without *paying* for her inalienable right—her liberty."

Mr. May in another place says of Harriet, that she deserves to be placed *first* on the list of American heroines, and then proceeds to give a short account of her labors, varying very little from that given in this book.

FUGITIVE SLAVE RESCUE IN TROY.

From the *Troy Whig*, April 28, 1859.

Yesterday afternoon, the streets of this city and West Troy were made the scenes of unexampled excitement. For the first time since the passage of the Fugitive Slave Law, an attempt was made here to carry its provisions into execution, and the result was a terrific encounter between the officers and the prisoner's friends, the triumph of mob law, and the final rescue of the fugitive. Our city was thrown into a grand state of turmoil, and for a time every other topic was forgotten, to give place to this new excitement. People did not think last evening to ask who was nominated at Charleston, or whether the news of the Heenan and Sayers battle had arrived—everything was merged into the fugitive slave case, of which it seems the end is not yet.

Charles Nalle, the fugitive, who was the cause of all

this excitement, was a slave on the plantation of B. W. Hansborough, in Culpepper County, Virginia, till the 19th of October, 1858, when he made his escape, and went to live in Columbia, Pennsylvania. A wife and five children are residing there now. Not long since he came to Sandlake, in this county, and resided in the family of Mr. Crosby until about three weeks ago. Since that time, he has been employed as coachman by Uri Gilbert, Esq., of this city. He is about thirty years of age, tall, quite light-complexioned, and good-looking. He is said to have been an excellent and faithful servant.

At Sandlake, we understand that Nalle was often seen by one H. F. Averill, formerly connected with one of the papers of this city, who communicated with his reputed owner in Virginia, and gave the information that led to a knowledge of the whereabouts of the fugitive. Averill wrote letters for him, and thus obtained an acquaintance with his history. Mr. Hansborough sent on an agent, Henry J. Wall, by whom the necessary papers were got out to arrest the fugitive.

Yesterday morning about 11 o'clock, Charles Nalle was sent to procure some bread for the family by whom he was employed. He failed to return. At the baker's he was arrested by Deputy United States Marshal J. W. Holmes, and immediately taken before United States Commissioner Miles Beach. The son of Mr. Gilbert, thinking it strange that he did not come back, sent to the house of William Henry, on Division Street, where he boarded, and his whereabouts was discovered.

The examination before Commissioner Beach was quite brief. The evidence of Averill and the agent was taken, and the Commissioner decided to remand Nalle to Virginia. The necessary papers were made out and given to the Marshal.

By this time it was two o'clock, and the fact began to be noised abroad that there was a fugitive slave in Mr. Beach's office, corner of State and First Streets. People in knots of ten or twelve collected near the entrance, looking at Nalle, who could be seen at an upper window. William Henry, a colored man, with whom Nalle boarded, commenced talking from the curb-stone in a loud voice to the crowd. He uttered such sentences as, "There is a fugitive slave in that office—pretty soon you will see him come forth. He is going to be taken down South, and you will have a chance to see him. He is to be taken to the depot, to go to Virginia in the first train. Keep watch of those stairs, and you will have a sight." A number of women kept shouting, crying, and by loud appeals excited the colored persons assembled.

Still the crowd grew in numbers. Wagons halted in front of the locality, and were soon piled with spectators. An alarm of fire was sounded, and hose carriages dashed through the ranks of men, women, and boys; but they closed again, and kept looking with expectant eyes at the window where the negro was visible. Meanwhile, angry discussions commenced. Some persons agitated a rescue, and others favored law and order. Mr. Brockway, a lawyer, had his coat torn for expressing his sentiments, and other *mêlées* kept the interest alive.

All at once there was a wild halloo, and every eye was turned up to see the legs and part of the body of the prisoner protruding from the second story window, at which he was endeavoring to escape.   Then arose a shout! "Drop him!" "Catch him!" "Hurrah!" But the attempt was a fruitless one, for somebody in the office pulled Nalle back again, amid the shouts of a hundred pairs of lungs.   The crowd at this time numbered nearly a thousand persons.   Many of them were black, and a good share were of the female sex.   They blocked up State Street from First Street to the alley, and kept surging to and fro.

Martin I. Townsend, Esq., who acted as counsel for the fugitive, did not arrive in the Commissioner's office until a decision had been rendered.   He immediately went before Judge Gould, of the Supreme Court, and procured a writ of habeas corpus in the usual form, *returnable* immediately.   This was given Deputy-Sheriff Nathaniel Upham, who at once proceeded to Commissioner Beach's office, and served it on Holmes.   Very injudiciously, the officers proceeded at once to Judge Gould's office, although it was evident they would have to pass through an excited, unreasonable crowd.   As soon as the officers and their prisoner emerged from the door, an old negro, who had been standing at the bottom of the stairs, shouted, "Here they come," and the crowd made a terrific rush at the party.

From the office of Commissioner Beach, in the Mutual Building, to that of Judge Gould, in Congress Street, is less than two blocks, but it was made a regular battlefield.   The moment the prisoner emerged from the doorway, in custody of Deputy-Sheriff Upham, Chief of Police Quin, Officers Cleveland and Holmes, the crowd made one grand charge, and those nearest the prisoner seized him violently, with the intention of pulling him away from the officers, but they were foiled ; and down First to Congress Street, and up the latter in front of Judge Gould's chambers, went the surging mass. Exactly what did go on in the crowd, it is impossible to say, but the pulling, hauling, mauling, and shouting, gave evidences of frantic efforts on the part of the rescuers, and a stern resistance from the conservators of the law. In front of Judge Gould's office the combat was at its height. No stones or other missiles were used ; the battle was fist to fist. We believe an order was given to take the prisoner the other way, and there was a grand rush towards the West, past First and River Streets, as far as Dock Street. All this time there was a continual *mêlée.* Many of the officers were hurt—among them Mr. Upham, whose object was solely to do his duty by taking Nalle before Judge Gould in accordance with the writ of habeas corpus. A number in the crowd were more or less hurt, and it is a wonder that these were not badly injured, as pistols were drawn and chisels used.

The battle had raged as far as the corner of Dock and Congress Streets, and the victory remained with the rescuers at last. The officers were completely worn out with their exertions, and it was impossible to continue their hold upon him any longer. Nalle was at liberty. His friends rushed him down Dock Street to the lower ferry, where there was a skiff lying ready to start. The fugitive was put in, the ferryman rowed off, and amid the shouts of hundreds who lined the banks of the river, Nalle was carried into Albany County.

As the skiff landed in West Troy, a negro sympathizer

waded up to the waist, and pulled Nalle out of the boat. He went up the hill alone, however, and there who should he meet but Constable Becker! The latter official seeing a man with manacles on, considered it his duty to arrest him. He did so, and took him in a wagon to the office of Justice Stewart, on the second floor of the corner building near the ferry. The justice was absent.

When the crowd on the Troy bank had seen Nalle safely landed, it was suggested that he might be recaptured. Then there was another rush made for the steam ferry-boat, which carried over about 400 persons, and left as many more—a few of the latter being soused in their efforts to get on the boat. On landing in West Troy, there, sure enough, was the prisoner, locked up in a strong office, protected by Officers Becker, Brown and Morrison, and the door barricaded.

Not a moment was lost. Up stairs went a score or more of resolute men—the rest "piling in" promiscuously, shouting and execrating the officers. Soon a stone flew against the door—then another—and bang, bang! went off a couple of pistols but the officers who fired them took good care to aim pretty high. The assailants were forced to retreat for a moment. "They 've got pistols," said one. "Who cares?" was the reply; "they can only kill a dozen of us—come on." More stones and more pistol-shots ensued. At last the door was pulled open by an immense negro, and in a moment he was felled by a hatchet in the hands of Deputy-Sheriff Morrison; but the body of the fallen man blocked up the door so that it could not be shut, and a friend of the prisoner pulled him out. Poor fellow! he might well say, "Save me from my friends." Amid the pulling and hauling, the iron had cut his arms, which were bleeding profusely, and he could hardly walk, owing to fatigue.

He has since arrived safely in Canada.

THE END.